# Finding My Faith

## By Kevin Harrington

**Truth**
Publications

Taking His hand,
helping each other home.

ISBN 10: 1-58427-528-6

ISBN 13: 978-1-58427-528-2

Truth Publications, Inc.
CEI Bookstore
220 S. Marion St., Athens, AL 35611
855-492-6657
sales@truthpublications.com
www.truthbooks.com

# Table of Contents

Dedicated

to my wife

and best friend,

Brooke

# Preface

I remember offering my very first devotional talk when I was a sophomore at Florida College. Until that point, I had done very little in regard to public worship. I had never taught a Bible class, never offered a public prayer, and especially never given a talk in front of a large group of people. At this point in my spiritual journey, I was young and dumb. I knew my Scriptures from years of attending Bible studies, but I had never been asked to talk about those Scriptures. I remember being surrounded by about a hundred or more students and all eyes were on me. I spent the next several minutes nervously talking about my topic for the night ("Blessed are those who mourn," Matt. 5:4), but what happened after is what truly catapulted me on an amazing spiritual journey.

Several students and friends came up to me after the devotional was over and told me, "Good job!" Only one came up to me and said, "Thank you. I needed to hear those words tonight." How did the words of a young, inexperienced Christian help someone? A little twenty-minute talk touched someone so deeply, it moved the person to come to me with tear-filled eyes to say, "Thank you." Then I realized it wasn't my words that moved that soul, it was God's words. His words filled this person's heart and made him feel inspired and encouraged. That's when I made the decision to become a preacher and teacher of God's word. My faith was new and weak, but I was determined to grow into a diligent student of the Bible.

There is power in what God says. There is healing in the pages of the Bible. Salvation is found only in Jesus and Jesus is found in Scripture. I wanted to help people find the power of God to heal them of their sins through Jesus Christ. I didn't want to preach lessons that make people say, "Good job," I wanted to help people find their purpose in life through their faith.

# Finding My Faith

My hope for this book is that you too will find a way to strengthen your faith. All of us are at different crossroads in our spiritual journey. Some people have followed Christ's footsteps for their entire lives and have a firm understanding of their Bibles and their faith. Others are struggling to find meaning and hope in God's words. While others have never picked up a Bible and know nothing about it. My prayer is that this book will be a blessing to all who are seeking to grow in their faith.

Those new to the Bible will find beneficial information as you begin to understand what the pages of Scripture mean. If you have questions about certain abbreviations or how to look up the Scriptures you read in this book, please see the page of abbreviations after this Preface to help you as you study. Those who are struggling can deepen their understanding of God's plan for love and salvation. If you are strong in the faith, you too can read these pages and have a better appreciation for what you were taught so long ago (and maybe you can also learn something new).

This book is designed with study questions at the end of each chapter to help you dig deeper in your spiritual journey. Some may choose to read this book alone, while others may choose to use it in a small group Bible study or even in a congregational setting. Either way, these questions will help you ask thought provoking questions to deepen your faith in God.

I want to thank several people for helping this book become a reality:

- My wife, Brooke, is my constant source of inspiration. She has taught me more about faith, love, and mercy than anyone I know.

- My parents who dedicated their lives to making sure I was fundamentally grounded in God's precious words.

- Each Bible class teacher I had growing up. They were volunteers who loved me enough to take the time to bring God's word to life.

- The men who taught me about preaching the gospel. Scott Vifquain, Marty Pickup, and Roger Shouse are all men I admire deeply.

- My professors at Florida College. You had to deal with an immature young man, but your knowledge and encouragement couldn't have come at a better time.

# Preface

- Those of you who read this book in its beginning stages. It was a rough and tedious read, but with your help it became the book you see today.

- The shepherds at Marion Street Church of Christ are the ones that encouraged me to write this book. I first taught this as a Bible class to the congregation at Marion Street and I was encouraged to write the words you are about to read. They have always supported my ideas and projects.

- The members at Marion Street Church of Christ. You continue to love, encourage and support me and my family. We love you all.

- Lastly, I want to thank YOU for taking the time to read this book. The fact you chose to pick up this book shows you want to learn more about God and His Word. It shows you have a heart that is seeking knowledge.

My hope is that this book will aid you on your journey to find and strengthen your faith. The Devil is real and powerful. Our one hope of defeating him is through our faith in Jesus Christ. I pray no matter where you find yourself on your spiritual path, you can consider yourself stronger in your faith by the end of these pages. God bless you on your journey.

# Abbreviations of Books of the Bible

The following abbreviations of Biblical books are used throughout this book. A Scripture references points a reader to the location of a passage within a given book of the Bible and the verse or verses where it can be found. They can be read as follows:

(Matt. 1:1) = (The Book of Matthew, chapter 1, verse 1)

### Old Testament

Gen. = Genesis
Exod. = Exodus
Lev. = Leviticus
Num. = Numbers
Deut. = Deuteronomy
Josh. = Joshua
Judg. = Judges
Ruth = Ruth
1 Sam. = 1 Samuel
2 Sam. = 2 Samuel
1 Kings = 1 Kings
2 Kings = 2 Kings
1 Chron. = 1 Chronicles
2 Chron. = 2 Chronicles
Ezra = Ezra
Neh. = Nehemiah
Esth. = Esther
Job = Job
Psa. = Psalms
Prov. = Proverbs

Eccl. = Ecclesiastes
S. of Sol. = Song of Solomon
Isa. = Isaiah
Jer. = Jeremiah
Lam. = Lamentations
Ezek. = Ezekiel
Dan.= Daniel
Hos. = Hosea
Joel = Joel
Amos = Amos
Obad. = Obadiah
Jonah = Jonah
Mic. = Micah
Nah. = Nahum
Hab. = Habbakuk
Zeph. = Zephaniah
Hag. = Haggai
Zech. = Zechariah
Mal. = Malachi

# Abbreviations of Books of the Bible

**New Testament**

Matt. = Matthew
Mark = Mark
Luke = Luke
John = John
Acts = Acts of the Apostles
Rom. = Romans
1 Cor. = 1 Corinthians
2 Cor. = 2 Corinthians
Gal. = Galatians
Eph. = Ephesians
Phil. = Philippians
Col. = Colossians
1 Thess. = 1 Thessalonians
2 Thess. = 2 Thessalonians

1 Tim.  = 1 Timothy
2 Tim.  = 2 Timothy
Titus = Titus
Phile. = Philemon
Heb. = Hebrews
Jas. = James
1 Pet. = 1 Peter
2 Pet. = 2 Peter
1 John = 1 John
2 John = 2 John
3 John = 3 John
Jude = Jude
Rev. = Revelation

# Introduction

In a recent survey by Lifeway Research, it was found that 70% of teenagers who grow up in homes and churches who believe in Christ, will leave the faith after they graduate from high school.[1] That number is staggering. That means seven out of ten young people who grew up learning Christian morals and fundamentals will ditch everything they've been taught once they leave the home. How could this be? Weren't they taught the stories of the Bible? Should their parents have done a better job teaching and training them? Unfortunately, we have come to accept the fact that most young people will choose to go experience life and indulge in the temptations of the world. We compile lists of excuses for why Christian teens are deciding to leave their faith. We hope that one day they will decide to come back to the Lord, but until that happens, we are convinced that young people just "need to be young" and experience life for a while.

I just can't accept that. I was bothered when I heard the statistic that 70% of teens abandoned their faith in Jesus once they graduated high school. What shocked me even more is that this is not unique to teens. In a national directory put out by *21ˢᵗ Century Christian* called "The Churches of Christ in the United States" we can see that the number of congregations who identify themselves as churches of Christ has decreased by 10% since the year 2000 and overall attendance has decreased by over 12%.[2] This isn't just a young people problem; it's a problem for any who put their faith in Jesus Christ . Why does it have to be that way?

I sat down and started to brainstorm why so many people decided to abandon their faith. We typically blame these kinds of things on outside influences. We blame friends, schools, politics, and our society for brainwashing and influencing Christians away from the Lord, especially the young ones. For some reason, we excuse our young people when influenced by outside sources, but if I, as a grown adult, decide to murder someone and blame it on the influences of society; I would still find my-self in jail. At some point, we have to take responsibility for our own actions and decisions.

Daniel was in his young teens when he was taken away from his parents and carried away to a foreign country. In Babylon, he was forced to learn a new language, live a new lifestyle, and practice a new religion. However, Daniel "purposed in his heart" to serve God (Dan. 1:8). David was a young shepherd boy who was able to fight off a bear and lion, not to mention the giant he defeated. Jesus was only twelve when He was teaching in the synagogue and the people marveled at what He was teaching.

It's time we stop making excuses for our young people leaving the faith. I strongly believe that if properly taught and motivated, teens can make strong, Biblical decisions once they leave the care of mom and dad . . . and even before.

As I brainstormed how to make this happen, I talked with several parents of young teens and even interviewed people from all over the country. I found that in a typical church environment, kids are taught basic Bible stories from the time they are babies until their middle school years. Once they reach middle school, they are now thrust into the "do's and don'ts" of their faith. No sex, no drugs, no alcohol, etc. We start giving them the list of sins to avoid. I have found that teens rarely get the Biblical stories they used to get in their elementary school days and instead get more topical studies. I don't want to take anything away from the studies the teens typically get; I think they are much needed and appropriate.

However, I believe we have failed our teens in one area: We have not shown them the importance of making their faith their own. We teach them the Biblical stories and never show them the connection to their own spiritual lives. We teach the cute stories and then transition them to the "do's and don'ts" of Christianity, but never show them the reason we do or don't do certain things. We never bridge the gap between the stories and their real life applications. In short, we teach them the *what* of Christianity, but never teach them the *why*. Many teens and newer Christians have never been taught the fundamental principles of their faith. Why do they believe in God? Why should they believe in God? What do the Old Testament stories have to do with their faith? What's the point of staying faithful to God?

# Introduction

We all want our young Christians to make wise decisions, but are we giving them the tools to do so? Are we showing them the connection between what they've learned as young children and how to apply it as young adults? It's no wonder 70% of teens are falling away from their faith; they have never been motivated enough to understand their faith and make it their own. It has always been mom and dad's faith. It was the Bible class teacher or the preacher's faith. So, as soon as they are confronted with life's challenges and mom, dad, the Bible class teacher, or the preacher aren't there: they have no idea how to handle the situation on their own. Or what about when they are asked a question about their faith, but don't have mom and dad to answer for them? What if someone offers what appears to be sound advice or doctrine, but is actually far from truth? If our young people have not been properly taught, they can be carried away in a heartbeat. Or, if on their own for the first time in college, what if mom and dad aren't there to wake them up for Bible class or services? Is it important enough to them to set their own alarm and attend services? If their faith was never their own and only belonged to mom and dad, then the answer is, "No. It's not important to them. It was important to mom and dad." It's time we teach our young people not only to have faith, but to make it their own.

Sadly, even older Christians are not immune to the same problems. I recently taught the following chapters at the congregation where I minister and I can't begin to tell you how many people in their 50's, 60's, and even 70's told me, "I wish this was taught to me when I was in my teens and twenties." For years, congregations have dropped the ball in transitioning their young Christians into maturity. It's no wonder even adults are leaving the faith. They were never given the tools to succeed. They were given the facts of their parent's faith, but never told to make it their own. Likewise, new converts often fall along the wayside because we assume they should know what we know. We throw them to the wolves in our adult classes and tell them to fend for themselves. Christians and congregations all over this country are hurting and dying because we have not done an adequate job in building and strengthening our faith.

That is the point of this book. I want all people, younger and older Christians alike, to have an appreciation for the faith that they have. I want us all to understand why we believe in an awesome and all-powerful God. To do that, we first have to understand His word. I have found that many people don't fully understand God's word and its purpose. How can we have a strong faith in God if we don't fully understand the Bible and what it offers us?

I want to make one thing abundantly clear: this book will not hold all the answers. In fact, my goal is to only scratch the surface of the wealth of knowledge we can find in the Bible in hopes to motivate you to continue reading and studying to deepen your faith and understanding in the Bible. Not everything that can be said, will be said. There are men and women who are far more educated than me, who have written far better books on several of the topics this book will address.

This book has been broken down into two parts. Part one is "Understanding Your Faith." It will look at several important topics and questions about understanding your Bible, understanding the Old Testament in light of the New Testament, and understanding our relationship with God. Part two is "Using Your Faith." This is the more practical application behind our faith. Now that we understand God's word and the important role it plays in our lives, how do I use it? What does it mean to be a Christian? How do I make wise decisions? And most importantly, how do I use God's word to help others?

My hope is that you will use this book as a guide and a resource to strengthen and deepen your faith in God and your understanding of His word. I hope that you will share this book with younger Christians who are at a pivotal time in their lives as they figure out their faith. My prayer is that in some small way, this book will help encourage Christians not only to understand their faith but to use it to further the borders of God's Kingdom.

I believe if properly equipped with the love and understanding of God's word, we can all learn to fight the temptations of the world around us. Don't be the statistic. It's time to find your faith and make it your own.

# Part One: Understanding My Faith

# CHAPTER 1
# The Journey Begins

There I was, sitting in front of my computer screen, scanning over all the words that were popping up one after the other. It seemed like as soon as I finished reading one comment, another would pop up right below. Someone had posted a comment on Facebook about how homosexuality was not a sin. As these conversations typically go, people started weighing in with their own *opinions*. I had always thought that the answer was pretty straightforward. After all, the Bible says, "You shall not lie with a male as with a woman. It is an abomination" (Lev. 18:22, NKJV). It also says, "Do you not know that the unrighteous will not inherit the kingdom of God? Do not be deceived. Neither fornicators, not idolaters, nor adulterers, nor HOMOSEXUALS, nor sodomites . . . will inherit the kingdom of God" (1 Cor. 6:9-10, emphasis mine).

I had grown up in "the church." I attended Bible classes from the time I could sit in a little bucket seat. I grew up singing all the Bible songs that kids sing in Bible classes and I remember reciting my memory verses each week so I could put a gold star on my "Memory Verse Chart." As I grew older, I remember hearing countless sermons and Bible classes (especially in the Jr. High and High School classes) about all the hot-button issues that we deal with today: homosexuality, sex before marriage, drinking, drugs, and abortion among other topics. I had always taken the preacher's word that these things were a sin. As Christians, we aren't supposed to do these things and the people who participate in these activities are sinners.

However, as I sat in front of my computer screen, watching all these people offer their opinions on homosexuality, I couldn't help but think, "why don't these people understand?" Why, when the Bible speaks so clearly on certain topics, do people feel like their opinion is better than the Bible's? Why are there differing opinions at all? I had always been taught that the Bible was right and if you're against the Bible, then you're against God. Yet, it seems to me that a majority of the world we live in today has a different opinion than what the Bible says. I had to ask myself if it was me that didn't fully understand.

## QUESTIONING MY FAITH

As I read through the arguments on that Facebook feed, I was reading the typical arguments about how the Bible states that homosexuality is wrong. However, something I had never heard before were the opposing arguments. My Bible class teachers had always told me what the Bible said, but never the counterarguments. I remember reading a comment along the line of, "The Old Testament also says it's a sin to eat pigs and shellfish (Lev. 11:8, 10), but Christians eat it anyway. So how can you listen to the Bible on homosexuality, but not listen on pigs and shellfish?" Technically, the commenter was right. That's what the Bible says. The Bible also says we have to keep the Sabbath Day (Deut. 5:12), but I hadn't observed the Sabbath Day at all during my life. Was I contradicting myself as a Christian? Another commenter wrote, "Jesus never said 'Thou shall not be a homosexual.'" Again, he was right. Jesus never said that. In fact, Jesus didn't have much to say on homosexuality at all—but He had plenty to say on fornication (see chapter seven and nine for more information).

I did what any normal human being would do: I started to question my own faith. If I was wrong about homosexuality, about what else might I be wrong? Was what I was taught in Bible class wrong? If the majority of my friends and the majority of America thinks one way, should I think that way too? I had always assumed the Bible was accurate, but how could I be so sure when so many people seemed to think otherwise? People, who were much more educated than me had excellent arguments and explanations for why we don't need to follow *every* part of the Bible. Educated people, even highly religious people, were coming to conclusions that God wants us to be happy, even if that means we go against His words. This had contradicted everything I had ever been taught. I never questioned God's existence, love, or forgiveness; and I never questioned the accuracy of the Bible. I had read enough books and articles about how we got the Bible we have today. I knew the Bible was God's word inspired by the Holy Spirit (2 Tim. 3:16-17), but I questioned if it could be followed; and whether or not it *should* be followed.

# The Journey Begins

And it was at that moment, as a freshman in college, I knew what I had to do. Before that moment, my faith in God and the Bible was weak. My parents had done an outstanding job raising me to know the difference between right and wrong. They made sure I was in church and went to my Bible classes, but until that point I had never been tested. Sure, I had faced temptations in middle school and high school. Many times I gave in to those temptations, but those temptations never made me question my beliefs in the Bible. I had spent years obtaining Biblical knowledge; learning the books of the Bible, memorizing all the names of the apostles, and learning all the stories of Jesus. But even with all these years of studying, I never learned how to practically apply my knowledge.

Faith is defined as, "complete trust or confidence in someone or something."[1] A Christian puts his or her complete trust and confidence in God and the Bible. However, at this point in my life, my trust and confidence were starting to be questioned. The Bible defines faith as "the substance of things hoped for, the evidence of things not seen" (Heb. 11:1). The word "substance" can also be translated "confidence" and the word "evidence" can also be translated as "assurance."

I felt like my faith was always solid and built on Biblical truths. I felt like I was *confident* in Who and what I believed. I felt like I was *sure* about how I was living my life. Now that I was seeing counterarguments and other opinions, I wasn't quite sure of my faith.

I came to a stunning conclusion: my faith was weak because I hadn't made it my own. It was always my parent's faith, my preacher's, or my Bible class teacher's. I had just memorized a bunch of facts and verses, but I had not been convinced and convicted that they were true. And once I was convicted, I didn't know what to do with my Biblical knowledge. Was there a reason I learned all these Biblical facts? What was the purpose in learning all this information if I was going to ditch everything the moment opposition arose?

There I was, on my own for the first time. I had been taught the Bible, but I hadn't been taught the world's views on the Bible. I hadn't been instructed about how to handle different thoughts and opinions other than my own. How would I teach other people the Bible, if I didn't fully understand it myself? Modern churches are really good at teaching the Bible, but they often fail miserably at teaching the practical use of the Bible. Therein lies the problem in our young people today: they are not being taught how to use the Bible on a daily basis. They are not being taught how to battle against world views. They are not being taught how to use their faith to strengthen the people around them. And they are definitely not being taught to make their faith their own. All they are told is to take the preacher's, their parents, or their church's word that the things being taught are true.

I had always been taught Christian values and I had obeyed the gospel, but at that moment, I decided to make my faith my own. I needed to know more. I needed to find the truth. I needed to be sure and confident. I needed to start my journey to find my own faith.

**IT'S OKAY TO ASK QUESTIONS**

In school, my teachers would always say, "There is no such thing as a dumb question." Let's face it, as much as we've heard that said, we all cringe when someone asks a dumb question. I have learned there is a majority of people that feel like there are things that everyone should know. There are things that should be considered "common knowledge." And when someone does not have the "common knowledge" that you have, we wonder where they've been hiding their whole life.

If we are going to give the Bible an honest and in-depth study, we must assume that nothing is common knowledge. The moment we assume we know something is the moment we have let our opinion overtake God's word. Instead, we need to understand that it is okay to ask questions.

Listen to some of these scenarios in the Scriptures of some things we may consider common knowledge, but people needed help to understand:

- "It happened that while Jesus was praying in a certain place, after He had finished, one of His disciples said to Him, 'Lord, teach us to pray just as John also taught his disciples'" (Luke 11:1). We assume everyone should know how to pray, yet the apostles who followed Jesus on a daily basis didn't even know how. What was common knowledge to Jesus, was not to His apostles.

- Philip came upon an Ethiopian eunuch, he noticed the eunuch was studying from the prophet Isaiah. Philip's question was, "Do you understand what you are reading?"

(Acts 8:30). The eunuch's answer was, "Well, how could I, unless someone guides me?" (Acts 8:31).

- As the apostle Paul came to the city of Ephesus, he found some disciples and asked, "Did you receive the Holy Spirit when you believed?" The disciple's response was, "No, we have not even heard whether there is a Holy Spirit" (Acts 19:2-3).

There are instances all throughout the Bible where something was common knowledge to one person, but it wasn't to another. As you study the Bible do not be afraid to admit you don't know something, do not be afraid to ask questions, and most importantly, do not be afraid to seek council from someone. How will we ever expect to grow spiritually if we are not willing to ask questions and study God's word with an open and honest heart?

This may be difficult for some people because asking questions may make you discover something that is contrary to what you already believe. Asking questions will take you on a journey that many people don't want to take because they are comfortable with where they are. If that's the case, then maybe this book is not for you. As a Christian, you have the responsibility to "be diligent to present yourself approved to God as a workman who does not need to be ashamed, accurately handling the word of truth" (2 Tim. 2:15).

There is no such thing as a dumb question. Every spiritual question you ask has the potential to knock down walls and bring you closer to God. Just because something is common knowledge to someone else does not mean that it is for you; and there is nothing wrong with that. Everyone starts their spiritual journey at the beginning. We may not all start at the same time, but we all start at the same place. I encourage you, as you study God's word, to ask as many questions as you can and don't be satisfied until you have received a Biblical answer.

**FAST FORWARD**

The chapters that follow are questions and answers that helped me get to where I am today. Through my journey I attended a small Bible school called Florida College, in Temple Terrace, Florida. While in school, I "sat at the feet" of professors who had dedicated their lives to teaching and preaching the gospel of Jesus Christ. I was not always the best student, but it was in college I decided to dedicate my life to studying

# Finding My Faith

God's word. I had three preaching internships in which I learned what it meant to study the Bible and teach it effectively. I received my Bachelor of Arts in Biblical Studies from Florida College and have been preaching fulltime since then. During these past several years, I have come across some of the most brilliant and humble students of the Bible. I have gained mentors that people would be lucky to have in their "contact lists." I have asked questions and studied harder than I ever have in my early Christian years.

I bring this up because I want you to know where I've been. I want you to know the doubts I had and the questions I asked. I want you to know what I have learned, so that you can go teach someone else. Everything you will read in this book is not something that I have come up with on a whim. These are not my opinions, but the result of a careful study of God's word. In this book you will read my stories and illustrations that I have heard from men far smarter and far more educated than myself.

I am still young and still learning. However, I am confident in the answers that God's word has revealed. I look back over the past several years and I see the growth that I have had. While I have learned a lot from strong men and women of faith, it was ultimately God who allowed me to grow spiritually. Paul tells us that it is God who gives the increase (1 Cor. 3:7). If you are willing to finish this study, I can guarantee that you will have a healthier understanding of God's word and how to use it in your everyday life. Whether or not you follow it is up to you. I firmly believe that a proper understanding of God's word is essential to have the kind of faith Jesus talks about in Matthew where He says, "for assuredly, I say to you, if you have faith as a mustard seed, you will say to this mountain, 'Move from here to there,' and it will move; and nothing will be impossible for you" (Matt. 17:20).

Join me on my journey. Come see how I strengthened my faith in God and His word. And witness how I went from a weak Christian, to making my faith, my very own.

# The Journey Begins

## Chapter 1 Study Questions

1. Why do you think many young people start to question their faith as they enter into high school and college?

2. What's the difference between knowing Biblical facts and being convinced and convicted of those Biblical facts?

3. Why do you think churches are not teaching their young people how to practically apply God's word?

4. Have you ever asked a question about something that was considered "common knowledge" to someone else? How did it make you feel knowing that everyone knew something that you didn't? Explain how this made you feel about asking questions in the future.

5. If people are afraid to ask Biblical questions, how will they ever grow spiritually? What can you do to make sure people can come to you if they have Biblical questions?

# CHAPTER 2
# What Is "My Faith?"

My favorite movie growing up was *The Mighty Ducks.* Soon after the movie came out, the city of Anaheim, CA became the home of the new NHL team, The Mighty Ducks. My favorite movie became my favorite team, which then became the team I played for at 5 years old in a city rec league. I grew up going to The Pond in Anaheim to watch the Ducks play. We had some decent years and we had some pretty dismal years too. Once, in 2003 we made it to the Stanley Cup Finals. Unfortunately, we had to face the New Jersey Devils. They were a great team who punished their opponents. The Ducks managed to force a winner take all Game 7 in New Jersey. I knew the odds were stacked against my favorite team. The Ducks were the underdogs playing against the heavy favorite in their hometown. As I was discussing the game with a friend, I remember telling him that I didn't like our chances and we would most likely lose the game and the Stanley Cup. He then said, "You just have to have faith."

That is a phrase that we use in so many different areas of life. When something isn't going our way, "Just have faith." When someone is sick and we want them to get better, "Just have faith." When your favorite sports team is on the verge of winning a championship, "Just have faith." Most times, the sentiment behind that statement is telling us to stay positive because we never know what might happen. However, I have found that the same phrase is given in times of spiritual distress as well. Are you struggling spiritually? "Just have faith." Are you dealing with sin and temptation? "Just have faith." Are you watching a loved one suffer in health? "Just have faith."

A lot of times the preacher will give the "cure all" answer that a lot of our problems can be fixed if we just strengthen our faith. It's almost like faith is the answer to all of our problems. If you have enough faith,

# What Is "My Faith?"

you can do anything. If you have a strong enough belief, sicknesses can be cured, doubters can be corrected, and maybe even your sports team will win the championship. So, we teach our young kids that when they have faith in God, they will be able to withstand temptation. Unfortunately, I have known several people who have faith in God, yet still choose to follow a path of sin. That tells me that simply having faith is not the answer. I don't want to take anything away from having faith; after all, that is the point of this entire book. However, simply saying we have faith will do nothing for us spiritually if we haven't learned not only what to have faith in, but how to use our faith and make it our own.

## WHAT IS FAITH?

The Bible defines faith as "the substance of things hoped for, the evidence of things not seen" (Heb. 11:1, NKJV). A standard definition of faith is simply "a complete trust or confidence in someone or something" (*New Oxford American Dictionary*). Using the standard definition, it's easy to see why people offer the advice to "Just have faith" in certain situations. It's about having confidence and trust that something will happen (a sick person gets better, your teams wins, etc.). However, Biblical faith is much deeper than just having confidence. I have been confident in several situations that ended up not going my way. Confidence is a feeling we get when we want something to happen. I have faith or confidence that while I'm going through the intersection of a green light, the traffic coming across is stopped at a red light. I'm confident that the people will stop at the red light, but we all know that sometimes that doesn't happen. Some people run red lights. My faith or confidence in the red light only depends on the people who are willing to stop at the red light. What assurance do I have that someone will actually stop? None, really. However, Biblical faith is not just the feeling of confidence. Biblical faith takes our feeling of confidence and gives us assurance.

The Hebrew writer tells us that faith is substance and evidence of the things hoped for and not seen. Those two words *substance* and *evidence* are the difference makers between worldly faith and Biblical faith. With Biblical faith we have substance. We have proof, or evidence, in what we believe. As a Christian, there are three main areas in which, without confidence and assurance, our faith would crumble: faith in God, faith in Christ, and faith in God's plan.

# Finding My Faith

## FAITH IN GOD

The foundation of faith is built about a belief in God. Not *a god*, but *the* God. We read in Genesis 1:1, "In the beginning God created the heavens and the earth." There is only one true God. He was there from the beginning. He is our Creator. In fact, right after giving the definition of faith, the Hebrew writer says, "By faith we understand that the worlds were framed by the word of God, so that the things which are seen were not made of things which are visible" (11:3). Have we seen God? No. How do we know He exists? The Hebrew writer tells us that although God is not visible, the things that He made are. The world we live in is evidence of our Creator.

Paul wrote, "For since the creation of the world His invisible attributes are clearly seen, being understood by the things that are made, even His eternal power and Godhead, so that they are without excuse" (Rom. 1:20). God's invisible attributes are clearly seen in His creation. Have you ever stood on the beach and watched the waves crash all around you? Have you felt the cool breeze on a hot summer day? Have you seen the power of a tornado or hurricane? Have you seen the life cycle of plants, animals, and trees? Have you ever studied DNA? Have you ever witnessed child development and birth? When you stop and look at the world around you, you learn that just because we cannot see God, doesn't mean the evidence and substance are not there.

We could spend countless chapters on our faith in God and the evidence behind Him. I'm assuming if you are reading this book, you already believe in God. I'm assuming you don't doubt that He exists and He's the one, true God. However, maybe you are like several Christians who just need a reminder of Who we believe in and why. Throughout this book, we will look at more of the evidence of God through His Word and why understanding our Bibles will only give us more evidence and substance in the existence of our one, true God.

## FAITH IN CHRIST

If we call ourselves disciples of Christ (or Christians, Acts 11:26), we are literally calling ourselves "followers of Christ." It means we have faith that there was a man named Jesus, He was sent by God to redeem humanity from their sins, He died on the cross as a sacrifice for our sins, He rose from the dead after three days in the tomb, and now

# What Is "My Faith?"

He is reigning for all eternity. Being a follower of Christ means we will not only have faith and believe in these facts, but we will follow Him the way He asked us to. Jesus said, "If anyone desires to come after Me, let him deny himself, take up his cross daily, and follow Me" (Luke 9:23). He also said, "If you love Me, keep My commandments" (John 14:15).

If our faith in God is the foundation of our faith as Christians, then our faith in Christ is the structure built upon the foundation (see next chapter). Paul said he preached the gospel that Jesus was killed, buried, and raised from the dead (1 Cor. 15:1-4). We have evidence and substance that this happened because Jesus was seen by hundreds of eyewitnesses (1 Cor. 15:5-8). If we don't have faith in Christ, Paul tells us that our preaching is empty (15:14). Not only is our preaching empty, but he says, "your faith is empty" (15:14). Our faith means nothing without Christ.

Again, I'm assuming if you are reading this book, you already have this belief. Maybe it's weak, but it's there. My hope is that as we go throughout this study, you will be able to see God's great plan of love, redemption, and salvation. My hope is your faith in Christ will grow stronger as you see God's will through His word.

## FAITH IN GOD'S PLAN

Our belief in God and our belief in Christ are the fundamental building blocks of our faith. If you grew up going to Bible classes like me, all the stories you read about Abraham, Isaac, Joseph, David, Peter, Paul, etc. are all aimed at planting those seeds of faith in God and Christ. With many people, the issue is not their belief in a Creator and His Son, but what to do with their belief. How do we bridge the gap between the stories and the practical application?

The more people I talk to, the more I see where people are struggling in their faith. They understand the stories of the Old and New Testament, but they have never been taught what they mean to their lives today. What does Abraham, who lived more than 4,000 years ago have to do with my life today? What does David, who lived almost 3,000 years ago have to do with my faith? When we not only understand the *what* of our Scriptures, but also the *why*, then we can begin to cultivate a faith that can move mountains.

# Finding My Faith

A lot of people struggle with knowing their purpose in life. What is God's plan for me? Did you know most young people feel like they have no purpose in the church? Did you know that most young people who attend a church feel like an afterthought because they can't be useful to a congregation or to God's kingdom until they are in college or maybe even into young adulthood? It's no wonder why young people are flocking away from their faith. They don't feel wanted. They don't have a purpose. Typically, their purpose is to come on Sundays, put a smile on their faces, attend Bible class, and help move chairs when they are needed. Unfortunately for many people, this leads to spiritual apathy and eventually, spiritual death.

Part of having faith in God and Christ, is having faith in their plan. God said, "For I know the thoughts that I think toward you . . . thoughts of peace and not of evil, to give you a future and a hope" (Jer. 29:11). We have to get people to see that God has a purpose for our lives. He has a plan. We have a future and a hope. My faith in God is not just an empty belief in an all-powerful Creator, but it's the belief in His plan for my life. A few chapters later in Jeremiah 31 He says, "I will put my law in their minds, and write it on their hearts; and I will be their God, and they shall be My people" (Jer. 31:33). That's the same idea that is echoed in Revelation 21:1-5 when we see a picture of Heaven.

God's plan is for us to be in Heaven together with Him. The Lord wishes that no man should perish, "but that all should come to repentance" (2 Pet. 3:9). God's plan is for you to be in Heaven. Where is the assurance and substance of that? Well, look back at the previous section about our faith in Christ. He is our assurance. "For God so loved the world that He gave His only begotten Son, that whoever believes in Him should not perish but have everlasting life" (John 3:16). Faith in God means having faith in His Son, Jesus. Faith in Jesus means knowing that everlasting life is a reality.

## FINDING FAITH

So, where does all this faith come from? Paul told the Romans, "faith comes by hearing, and hearing by the word of God" (Rom. 10:17). Simply put: your faith will come from a steady diet of God's word. If we want our faith to grow, it means we will open our Bibles and see what God is trying to tell us. It means our Bibles will have to be taken off the shelf, pulled out of the drawer, and stop being used as a coffee table book. It means you will have to finally open that app on your phone or tablet. God's word needs to be heard and it needs to be read.

Sometimes I forget what a blessing it is to have God's word so easily available. The Bible is the most printed book in the history of mankind, yet it's often the most neglected. Through the next several chapters, we will take some time to get to know the purpose of our Bibles. Why are there two testaments? Why are there so many books? What's the purpose?

It's amazing what will happen to your faith when you open God's word and start reading it. All of a sudden, a mystical and distant god becomes real and personal. A doubted Christ becomes a guiding light. God's plan is seen from the very first pages and concludes with a picture of eternity on the last few pages. Through God's word, assurance is given, hope is nurtured, and faith begins to grow.

## FAITH IN ACTION

Once we have faith in God, Jesus, and the plan they have for us . . . what do we do with it? I don't think many would argue with the previous segments and what we're supposed to have faith in, yet where many people drop the ball is what to do with their faith once they have it.

Pew Research Center says that 89% of Americans identify themselves as Christians. That means they have a firm belief in God and His Son, Jesus. However, research also shows that only 51% of Americans attend a regular church service. I'm not saying just because someone attends church services means they have it all figured out spiritually, but it's usually an indicator of how seriously someone takes their faith. If 89% of Americans believe in God, why are only 51% regularly worshiping Him at a church service?[1]

If 89% of Americans believe in God, why do we still have so many problems in our society? Why is sin such an epidemic? Why are we so torn on issues like homosexuality, abortion, etc.? All of this tells me that faith alone is not the answer.

During His conclusion of the Sermon on the Mount, Jesus says, "Not everyone who says to Me, 'Lord, Lord,' shall enter the kingdom of heaven, BUT HE WHO DOES THE WILL OF MY FATHER IN HEAVEN" (Matt. 7:21, emphasis mine). Jesus made it very clear that He expected His followers not just to have faith, but also to follow the will of God. I wonder how many people today are saying "Lord, Lord," yet refuse to open His word and figure out what God expects of them. I wonder how many people today are saying "Lord, Lord," yet only follow Jesus in name only. I wonder how many people today are saying, "Lord, Lord," yet have never taken the time to make their faith their own and start using their faith according to God's will.

Sometimes we idolize the men and women of the Bible stories, but can I say something that might sound a little different? There is nothing special about the men and women in the Bible. The "main Bible characters" were normal people just like you and me. They were shepherds, farmers, tentmakers, fishermen, tax collectors, men, women, rich, and poor. They came from all different walks of life. What made them special is what they were able to do with their faith in God.

When you read through Hebrews 11, you will see exactly what I mean. Nineteen times the Hebrew writer said, "By faith. . . ." Why was Moses able to stand in front of Pharaoh, cross the Red Sea and lead the people of Israel? By faith. Why was Rahab able to hide the spies and be saved from the destruction of her city? By faith. Why were these normal people able to subdue kingdoms, work righteousness, stop the mouths of lions, quench the violence of fire, escape the edge of the sword, and be valiant in battle? By faith.

These ordinary people became extraordinary because they were willing not only to have faith, but put their faith into action. They were willing to take the difficult, but necessary steps to serve God the way He is meant to be served. They were willing to look past the doubters and see the evidence and assurance of God and His plan.

**MAKING IT MINE**

The last step in understanding where faith comes from and what to do with it is the most difficult. I was taught about God, Jesus, and their plan from a very young age. I sat in Bible classes and attended weekly worship services. I knew the Bible stories by heart. For the longest time, it was the faith of my parents. They are the ones that woke me up on Sunday morning. They are the ones that drove me to our weekly Bible studies. They are the ones that pushed me to do my Bible class work. However, at some point, each person will come to a crossroads in his or her spiritual journey. At some point in your life, you will have to ask yourself, "Whose faith is it?"

# What Is "My Faith?"

Listen to these interactions in Scripture:

- "Then they said to the woman, 'Now we believe, not because of what you said, for we ourselves have heard Him and we know that this is indeed the Christ, the Savior of the world'" (John 4:42).

- "Now as they went down the road, they came to some water. And the eunuch said, 'See, here is water. What hinders me from being baptized?' Then Philip said, 'If *you* believe with all YOUR heart, you may'" (Acts 8:36-37, emphasis mine*)*.

- "These were more fair-minded than those in Thessalonica, in that they received the word with all readiness, and searched the Scriptures daily to find out whether these things were so" (Acts 17:11).

All through Scripture, people were encouraged to make their faith their own. They studied Scriptures, they asked questions, and they came to conclusions. But their conclusions were their own. Their faith belonged to them. It was personal. Yes, someone taught them and shared the message of Jesus with them, but at the end of the day, the decision to believe was up to the individual.

Now the decision is yours. Whose faith do you have? If you are reading some of these things and thinking, "I've always just believed what mom, dad, Bible class teachers, or my preacher have always taught," you are not alone. Maybe you've grown up in a church or denomination and you've always "taken their word for it." Thousands who consider themselves Christians have faith but have never taken the crucial and important step of making it their own. You may go through this book and question everything you've been taught. You may start seeing things from a different perspective. You may come to the conclusion that what you were taught by your parents, preacher, or church is not what God's word teaches. When you make the choice to make your faith your own, you are making the choice not only to say, "Lord, Lord," but also to say, "His will be done."

Unfortunately, the Ducks lost Game 7. We lost the Stanley Cup and very few people will even remember they were the number two team in the world in 2003. Thankfully, in 2007 we had another shot at the

# Finding My Faith

Stanley Cup. I was actually at the game when we won it! I understood the sentiment behind what my friend was saying when he said, "have faith." He was saying, "Be positive; you never know what will happen." That's the problem with faith today. A faith in God is not supposed to be, "you never know what will happen." Faith in God is based on assurance and evidence. Faith is meant to be strong and dependable. Are you ready to find this kind of faith? It starts with what Paul said, "faith comes by hearing, and hearing from the word of God" (Rom. 10:17).

Get your Bibles ready. It's time to find our faith.

# What Is "My Faith?"

## Chapter 2 Study Questions

1. Explain the difference between the world's definition of faith and the Biblical definition of faith.

2. Can you think of any substance and evidence that have strengthened your faith in God? If you can't think of anything, take some time and look at the world around you. See if you can find any evidence of God?

3. Why is it so important not only to have faith in God and Christ, but also their plan?

4. Can you think of an example in Scripture of someone who had faith but didn't use it? What was the outcome? Compare that with Hebrews 11. What do you think God expects out of those people who have faith?

5. Explain the difference between having the faith of "someone else" versus having your own faith. Why is it so important to make your faith your own?

# CHAPTER 3
# Building a Castle

As I started talking with more people about the Bible, I found that very few people respected the Bible as God's word. Most people I came in contact with would say they were actual Christians or they believed in God, but when it came to following the words in the Bible, they would much rather live by their own set of rules. Sadly, too many people have made this choice.

The Center for the Study of Global Christianity estimated that in the year AD 1900 there were 1,600 different types of churches who considered themselves "Christian." That's a total of 1,599 more than there were at the time Paul wrote, "There is ONE body and ONE Spirit, just as you were called in ONE hope of your calling; ONE Lord, ONE faith, ONE baptism; ONE God and Father of all, who is above all, and through all, and in you all" (Eph. 4:4-6, NKJV; emphasis mine). The apostles only recognized *one* kind of church and that was the church that followed the doctrine of Jesus Christ (see Acts 2:40-47). However, by AD 1900, there were an estimated 1,600 different churches who considered themselves "Christian." One hundred years later in the year 2000, there were an estimated 34,000 different types of churches who considered themselves "Christian." In 2012 that number jumped to 43,000.[1]

Obviously, over the past 2,000 years since Christ established His church His word has not changed, so what has changed? There are two major factors that have contributed to this dramatic change. First (and the main focus of this chapter), people do not have a healthy respect for God's word and its authority. Second (and the main focus of later chapters), people do not know what it truly means to be a Christian.

## BUILDING A CASTLE

As I finished my senior year at Florida College, I moved to New Albany, Indiana to work with Charlestown Road Church of Christ. The

# Building a Castle

preacher I worked with would change my life forever. Roger Shouse not only became a mentor, but also a father figure and friend. He shared with me one of the easiest, yet most convincing illustrations to understand the importance of following God's word. I felt I had always understood God's word, but hearing this illustration helped me put into words what I had always been taught.

Imagine you and I went on a vacation to Europe. As we are traveling the beautiful countryside, we see an ancient medieval castle in the distance. As we approach the castle we are struck by its beauty, culture, and detail. We think to ourselves, "America doesn't have any castles like this." So, we decide to build an exact replica of this castle back home. Money is no object, so let's get to work.

If we are going to build this castle in America, we will need a few things. First, we will need similar *materials*. We cannot build an ancient medieval castle with aluminum siding and bricks. It won't look the same or be the same. We need the same material they used back then. Second, we will need similar *tools*. To give the castle the shape and texture of the original, we need to use the tools the original builders used. Third, we will need to follow the *blueprint*. The blueprint is what tells us exactly how to build the castle.

Once we have our materials, our tools, and our blueprint, we get to work. As we are building our replica castle, we start seeing some things that could use some upgrading. In ancient times, they didn't have running water. No running water means that we will need to use the restroom outside in an outhouse, it means we will have to fetch our own water to cook and bathe, and it also means that any time we need hot water, we will have to boil it ourselves. Let's go ahead and run some plumbing into our castle. Back then, they used fire as their only source of light and heat. I don't know about you, but I am going to need some air conditioning in the summer and some heat in the winter. I will also need lights to see. We might as well run the castle with electricity. Speaking of electricity, what about a kitchen? In ancient times they just cooked over a fire. I really enjoy using an oven, stove, and microwave. Let's update the kitchen a little bit to make sure we can cook a proper meal.

By the time the castle is finished we will have made so many changes that any person with common sense will be able to see *the castle we made is nothing like the original.* It may look similar, but it's not the same. Sure, the changes we made were minor to the overall structure of the castle, but they completely changed the functionality. Here's the problem: we had a blueprint for what we should have built, but somewhere along the way we changed it.

Some might ask the question, "What's the big deal with making changes to the blueprint if it makes things easier or better?" The big deal is the fact that you set out to build one thing, a replica of the original castle, and at the end of the process you produced something very different. We didn't accomplish our goal. We changed the blueprint so much that the two castles are nothing alike.

## BUILDERS, NOT ARCHITECTS

Here is the problem we encountered while building our castle: we had a blueprint and chose not to follow it. In fact, we not only chose not to follow it, we chose to change it. There are people who spend several years in school learning how to design and develop buildings. They are called architects. Architects are the ones who tell us where to put windows, doors, walls, etc. They design buildings not only to look good, but to be structurally sound. They have the structural integrity of the building in mind when they place things in their desired spots. When an architect finishes a blueprint, he hands it off to the builders.

The builders are the ones in charge of taking the blueprint made by the architect and following every direction carefully. If the builder does his job, the building the architect designed and the building the builder builds will be the same. What if during the building process, a builder decides he doesn't like a wall where the architect put it in the blueprint? So, the builder removes the wall from the building process. By removing the wall, the builder has put the entire project at risk. What if that wall was a main support? What if that wall held plumbing or electrical? Because of the builder's decision to change something, a series of problems now presents itself. The architect has one job: design the building. The builder has one job: take the architect's design and build the building. Together, they can build something beautiful.

## GOD'S THE ARCHITECT, WE ARE THE BUILDERS

Remember our question at the beginning of the chapter? How did we get from *one* church in the New Testament to over 43,000 different

# Building a Castle

types of churches today? The answer is simple: we have too many people wanting to be the architects and not enough people trying to build what the architect has already given us. When you look at the illustration of the castle, it's quite clear who our architect is: God. Look at some of these terms and phrases in the Bible (emphasis mine).

- "... On this rock I will build MY CHURCH..." (Matt. 16:18)
- "All scripture is breathed out BY GOD..." (2 Tim. 3:16)
- "And he gave the apostles, the prophets, the evangelists, the shepherds and teachers, to equip the saints for the work of ministry, for BUILDING UP THE BODY OF CHRIST" (Eph. 4:11-12)
- "For no one can lay a foundation other than that which is laid, which is JESUS CHRIST" (1 Cor. 3:11)
- "... All the churches OF CHRIST send greetings" (Rom. 16:16)
- "... Shepherd the church OF GOD which He purchased with His own blood" (Acts 20:28)
- "For we are GOD'S fellow workers; you are GOD'S field, you are GOD'S building" (1 Cor. 3:9)
- "... I write so that you may know how you ought to conduct yourself in the HOUSE OF GOD, which is the CHURCH OF THE LIVING GOD, the pillar and ground of truth" (1 Tim. 3:15)

It's easy to see that Scripture very clearly states that God is the architect. "All scripture is breathed out by God..." (2 Tim. 3:16, ESV). He has given us the blueprint. He has given us what He expects out of His church and His people. Peter tells us "you also, as living stones, are being built up a spiritual house, a holy priesthood, to offer up spiritual sacrifices acceptable to God through Jesus Christ" (1 Pet. 2:5, NKJV). God is the architect and we are the builders. He has given the builders the blueprint on how to build the church that Christ established.

Unfortunately, over the years, too many people have decided they didn't want to be builders, but instead they wanted to be the architect. Over the last 2,000 years, people have made subtle changes to God's blueprint. Remember the castle? They have been moving walls, adding doors and windows, adding plumbing and electricity. Instead of literally adding doors, windows, and plumbing, people have added to the New Testament church musical instruments, supporting institutions, and many other things that aren't found in the blueprint. They have "removed walls" by not observing the Lord's Supper, moving worship to Saturdays *instead of* the first day of the week (Sunday), not baptizing for salvation, or by only meeting one or two days a year on "religious holidays." Before too long, the church that was established in the New Testament became a thing of the distant past. The Lord's church has been pulled and stretched in so many different directions that we have come to think thousands of different churches are sound, scriptural churches. When in reality, most of those 43,000 different types of churches are so far from God's original blueprint, they can't even see where they got off track.

We would do well to remember what Paul told the Corinthian church when he said, "For no one can lay another foundation other than that which is laid, which is Jesus Christ" (1 Cor. 3:11). If we are going to build the blueprint that God has given us, it is going to be by building upon the foundation that has already been laid by Jesus Christ. Paul and Peter both refer to Christ as the chief cornerstone (Eph. 2:20; 1 Pet. 2:6-7). A cornerstone is often referred to as a "foundation stone." It's the stone upon which the rest of the building is built. Christ is the church's cornerstone. He's our foundation. He's our authority.

## TIME TO BUILD

If we are going to be successful in building the Kingdom of God, we must do it His way. I think two major factors have contributed to people changing God's blueprint. First, people suffer from a serious case of selfishness. When God's kingdom becomes more about us than serving God the way He was meant to be served, we have lost our focus on what's truly important. The moment I look at God's blueprint and make changes to suit my wants and desires, I have left my job as a builder and have self-promoted myself to act as the architect. We will deal with this topic in later chapters when we discuss what it truly means to be a Christian. The second factor contributing to people changing God's blueprint is a lack of understanding of God's word. How can we begin to respect the authority of God's word and blueprint if we don't understand what we are reading? Builders cannot change the blueprints, but they sure have been trained on how to read and understand them. If we are not similarly trained in how to understand the Bible and its purpose, then we will never respect the authority of God.

Just like building the castle, if we are going to build the church of the New Testament, we must have three things: similar materials, similar tools, and the blueprint. We've already established that God, the

# Building a Castle

architect, has given us the blueprint. He has given us the Bible (God's word). Within the blueprint, God has shown us what materials and tools we should be using. We just need to know how to use the materials and tools that we are given.

After hearing this illustration of building a castle, it was easy to understand the necessity to follow the blueprint. For the first time, I saw the Bible as not just as an old book full of stories I learned while growing up in Bible classes, but as a blueprint for my life. It showed me how to act, how to speak, and how to live. I finally felt like there was a purpose to my life and the answers were somewhere in God's word. However, there were still many questions that needed to be answered. Do we follow the Old Testament, the New Testament, or both? What are testaments? What am I really supposed to be building according to God's blueprint?

Every person needs to realize something: if we don't understand the general makeup and concept of the Bible, we cannot be effective builders in the Lord's kingdom. I wanted to know more. I needed to know more. What is the Bible and what do all these ancient writings have to do with my life today?

## Chapter 3 Study Questions:

1.  Why do you think there are so many churches today?

2.  If you were going to build a replica of a medieval castle, what three things would you need? Why?

3.  What happened to the castle after we made our changes?

4.  What's the big deal with making changes to the blueprint if it makes things easier or better?

5.  What is the difference between being a builder and being an architect? Why is this important when it comes to God's word?

6.  Why do you think so many churches have gotten so far away from God's blueprint?

7.  What are the two factors contributing to God's blueprint being changed?

# CHAPTER 4
# Understanding the Bible

If I were to walk into your work one day and ask to see the instruction manual on how to do your job, it might be a pretty thick folder full of rules, regulations, tasks, and responsibilities. In the folder there would likely be everything I need to know to effectively do your job. What if I opened up the folder, turned to a random page, pulled out a random sentence or paragraph, read it, and suggested to you I now know exactly how to do your job? Would you believe me? I'm sure you would look at me and laugh, knowing in order to fully understand and comprehend your job, it would take much more than reading one sentence or paragraph about your position.

Unfortunately, this is exactly what people do with the Bible. The Bible is neatly divided up into books, chapters, and verses so that we can easily find passages we want to read. A many people with whom I have come in contact know the Bible consists of the Old and New Testaments. They know that the Old Testament has thirty-nine different books and the New Testament has twenty-seven different books making a total of sixty-six books in the Bible. (If you didn't know that, it's easy to open up to the Table of Contents of any Bible and simply see the breakdown and order of the books.)

The thing that I find interesting is that many people understand the breakdown of the Bible, but they have no idea how it all fits together. What does the Old Testament have to do with the New Testament? Why do we still read the old if we have the new? If Jesus is so important, why doesn't He show up until over halfway through the book? What are "the writings" or the "prophets" and what is their purpose? Very few people actually understand the Bible, but most people feel like they can use it to say whatever it is they want to say. It would be exactly like trying to put a puzzle together without looking at the picture on the front of the box. You have all the pieces, understand that they are all supposed to fit together, but you have no idea what the end result is supposed to look like.

## KNOWING VS. UNDERSTANDING

In a recent study, Pew Research Center found that atheists (those who don't believe in God) and agnostics (those who "don't know" if God exists or not) scored higher on a basic Bible knowledge test than all but two religious groups.[1] Yes, you read that right: people who don't believe in God and people who doubt the existence of God have more Bible knowledge than the vast majority of people who actually believe in God. (*If you're curious, the only two religious groups that scored higher were Mormons and Jews).* Here's what that statistic proves: just because you know your Bible, doesn't mean you understand it. The test showed that atheists and agnostics knew the Bible. However, the very fact that they don't believe in God or doubt His existence shows me they have no idea what it all actually means.

A majority of the "spiritual debates" happen today because of this very reason: people like to think they know more than they really do. Just like you would think it foolish if I walked into your work, read a sentence of your job description, and assumed I can now do your job; it is foolish for someone to think he or she knows the Bible by just picking out one verse and using it in an argument or debate. Satan used Scripture when he tried to tempt Jesus in the wilderness, but Satan didn't fully understand the meaning of the Scriptures he was using (Matt. 4:1-11). Unfortunately, Satan has influenced many people to use that same tactic today.

There are thousands of people who will quote Scripture, but they have no idea what the Scripture actually means. People will throw Bible verses into all different kinds of arguments and conversations and our first reaction is to think that they know their Bible. However, upon further examination, you can tell a lot about someone's knowledge in the Scripture by how they use it in everyday situations.

How do we go from someone who "knows" the Bible to someone who "understands" the Bible? There is a major difference between those two words. I "know" that you need gas to make a vehicle run, however I don't "understand" how gas actually makes the vehicle work. I fill up my tank when it's empty and assume that the car will start. How does it actually work? I have no clue, but other people do. So, when my car doesn't work, I go to a mechanic. I "know" there are stars, planets, and solar systems in our universe. Do I "understand" how they all work and interact? Absolutely not. However, there are people who do, so we listen to their expert advice.

It is similar with the Bible. Anyone can pick up a Bible, turn to a random page and "know" what the Bible says. However, do we understand what we are reading? In Acts 8, Philip came across an Ethiopian Eunuch who was reading a portion of Isaiah. Philip approached the eunuch and asked, "Do you understand what you are reading?" The eunuch replied, "How can I, unless someone guides me?" (Acts 8:30-31, NKJV). He was reading Scripture and knew what it said but needed someone to guide him to understanding.

In a verse that we mentioned in a previous chapter, Paul told Timothy to "be diligent to present yourself approved to God, a worker who does not need to be ashamed, rightly dividing the word of truth" (2 Tim. 2:15). First, we must be diligent in our study of God's word. We must never stop studying and reading. Spiritual growth only takes place when we have securely planted ourselves in God's word.

Second, we must not be ashamed of the truth we find in Scripture. When we find ourselves in a situation where the majority of the people are against God's word, that doesn't mean we join in with the crowd. It means we boldly take our stand for truth. Paul says, "For I am not ashamed of the gospel of Christ, for it is the power of God to salvation for everyone who believes" (Rom. 1:16).

Third, we must rightly divide the word of truth. This means we have the responsibility as Bible students to accurately handle God's word. The term "rightly divide" is an ancient term used in farming. When a farmer was plowing his field, he was to "rightly divide" his field, plow in straight lines, so he could plant his crop. We must keep God's word straight and accurate. This means that we not only know God's word, but we understand and properly use God's word in context.

## THE BREAKDOWN OF THE BIBLE

In order to understand the Bible and use it properly, we must first understand the breakdown of the Bible. As stated previously, most people know the Bible is made up of sixty-six books. In fact, that's what the word "Bible" means. The English word "Bible" comes from the Latin word *biblia* which means, "the books." So, the basic definition of the Bible is "a collection of books"—sixty-six to be exact.

Those sixty-six books are broken up into two sections: the Old Testament and the New Testament. But what is a testament? It's not a word we use in our everyday vocabulary and is often just described as a "Bible word." Although we don't use the word "testament" in our everyday vocabulary, the meaning is something we very much understand.

The word "testament" comes from the Greek word *diatheke* and means, "covenant." A covenant is an agreement. We see covenants every day in our modern world. One of the most popular covenants we see is the marriage covenant. When a couple is married, they make an agreement, or covenant, with each other and God to stay faithful to one another "till death do us part." In that scenario, death breaks the covenant. We also see covenants in business deals when a contract is signed. This signifies that there is a covenant or agreement between two parties. Another popular covenant we see today is someone's "last will and testament." This is where someone who is dying can legally specify who receives his possessions and property upon his death. It's a signed document (covenant) which makes it a binding contract.

So, what does all this have to do with the Bible? God made several different covenants with His people. However, there are two main covenants that drive the story of the Bible forward: the covenant with Moses and the "New Covenant" that was put into place by Jesus. We have simplified the covenants by calling them the "Old" and the "New."

Just as a disclaimer, we will not be dealing with "covenants" in depth in this book. If you are interested in reading more about covenants in Bible times, especially the covenant we have with Christ, I suggest you read the book *Inside Out: The New Covenant Written on the Heart* by Mike Wilson (CreateSpace Independent Publishing Platform, 2015).

However, in the next chapter, I will be explaining the deeper significance of God's covenants with Moses and the New Testament brought by Jesus. We will even briefly look at a covenant made between God and Abraham, but before we get too far ahead of ourselves, I think it's necessary to understand the breakdown of the Bible. When you open your Bible and see all these different books, chapters, and verses, what are you really looking at? Where are you when you turn

# Understanding the Bible

to Jeremiah? Who is Ezra? Why are their four Johns, but one of them is toward the beginning of the New Testament while the other three are pushed to the end? Understanding the breakdown of the Bible will help us in the next chapter when we discuss the purpose of the testaments.

## THE OLD TESTAMENT

I'm a firm believer that before you can understand the *purpose* of the Old Testament, you first have to understand the *makeup* of the Old Testament. The Old Testament is made up of thirty-nine books. The book of Job is considered to be the oldest of the books and Malachi the last to be written. All the books of the Old Testament span approximately from 1500 BC (maybe earlier depending on when Job was written) to 400 BC. That's a period of over 1,100 years.

If these books were written over a period of 1,100 years, then I think it's safe to say that more than one person had a hand in writing these books. Below is a breakdown of who wrote each book.

- Genesis, Exodus, Leviticus, Numbers, Deuteronomy – **Moses**
- 1 Kings, 2 Kings, Jeremiah, Lamentations – **Jeremiah**
- 1 Chronicles, 2 Chronicles, Ezra – **Ezra**
- Ecclesiastes, Song of Solomon – **Solomon**
- Psalms had various writers (each number represents an estimate of the number of Psalms each person authored) – **David** (75; see Acts 4:25 and Hebrews 4:7 regarding Psalms 2 and 95), **Asaph** (12), **Sons of Korah** (11), **Solomon** (2), **Moses** (1), **Ethan** (1), **Heman** – with Korah (1), **Unkonwn** (48)
- Proverbs had various writers – **Solomon, Agur, Lemuel**

There are some books whose authorship is uncertain, but below are the more "popular" candidates.

- Judges, Ruth – **Samuel**
- 1 Samuel – **Samuel/Gad/Nathan**
- 2 Samuel – **Gad/Nathan**
- Job – **Moses**
- Esther – **Mordecai**

Below is a list of the writers whose book is titled after themselves.

- **Joshua, Nehemiah, Isaiah, Ezekiel, Daniel, Hosea, Joel, Amos, Obadiah, Jonah, Micah, Nahum, Habakkuk, Zephaniah, Haggai, Zechariah, Malachi**

That's over thirty different authors just for the Old Testament. If you include the New Testament authors, that number jumps closer to forty. Part of what makes the Bible so special is that the message stays the same no matter the time between writings and the number of authors. I believe this is due in large part to what we read in 2 Timothy 3:16, "All Scripture is given by inspiration of God. . . ." If all Scripture is given by God, then the ultimate and overall author is God. His message stays clear and constant. He is only using the men to write down the message so it can be available to all generations.

There is a reason we call the Bible "God's word." It's because it is actually the words of God. The words were given by God in various ways. God communicated with His people through law, sermons, prophecy, songs, laments, dreams, visions, parables, proverbs, and even oral communication with certain individuals. All of these styles of communication through a time period of 1,100 years are right at our fingertips. We are literally reading the words of God. How incredible is that?

Most people assume the books are listed in chronological order. A lot of them are, but the way they are arranged in our Bibles is for a specific reason. They are grouped by different types of writings. If we were to list them chronologically, we would most likely have to put Job first and Malachi last. Well, Malachi is listed last in our Old Testaments, but Job is listed as number eighteen. We would also have to move Ezra, Nehemiah, and Esther (which are listed before Job at numbers 15-17) down toward the bottom of the list (and don't even get me started on the Prophets).

The books of the Bible are actually listed by subject matter and not chronologically. This mirrors the arrangement of the Septuagint, which is the Greek translation of the Old Testament that was made a few hundred years before Christ. The Old Testament books can actually be broken down into five subjects:

1. **Law** – Genesis, Exodus, Leviticus, Numbers, Deuteronomy
2. **History** – Joshua, Judges, Ruth, 1 Samuel, 2 Samuel, 1 Kings, 2 Kings, 1 Chronicles, 2 Chronicles, Ezra, Nehemiah, Esther
3. **Wisdom/Poetry** – Job, Psalms, Proverbs, Ecclesiastes, Song of Solomon
4. **Major Prophets** – Isaiah, Jeremiah, Lamentations, Ezekiel, Daniel

5. **Minor Prophets** – Hosea, Joel, Amos, Obadiah, Jonah, Micah, Nahum, Habakkuk, Zephaniah, Haggai, Zechariah, Malachi

   ** *I think it's important to note the two kinds of prophets here. The difference between "Major" and "Minor" is not the content or the message of the book but based on the size of the book. In ancient times, these were all written on scrolls. A Major Prophet would take a whole scroll for the entire writing whereas all twelve Minor Prophets could fit together onto one scroll.*

We have to remember why the books were put into this order. When we open our Bibles, we see a lot of chapters and verses. If your preacher tells you to open your Bible to Psalms 22:2, it would be very easy to find the book of Psalms. Then you find chapter 22. Then you find verse 2. This wasn't always the case. Chapters were not introduced until AD 1227 by someone named Stephen Langton. And they weren't put into the Bible until AD 1382 when the Wycliffe English Bible started using them. Verses came even later when the Old Testament was divided in AD 1448 and the New Testament in AD 1555.

Before chapters and verses, the entire book would have to be searched to find a particular section that you might be looking for. To make things easier to find, the books of the Bible were arranged into the above sections.

We will have more to say about the purpose of the Old Testament later on, but now let's take a look at the New Testament.

**THE NEW TESTAMENT**

More emphasis is probably put on the New Testament than the Old. We know about Jesus and His followers and we know they are from the New Testament, but very few people actually know what's in the New Testament. Jesus is probably the most popular name to come out of the New Testament, but He's only in the first four books, the first chapter of the Acts, and different scenes in the book of Revelation. So, what's the purpose for the rest of the New Testament?

The events of the New Testament range approximately from year 6 BC through around AD 70-97. The reason for the wide range is because there is a lot of speculation on when Jesus was born and when the book of Revelation was written. Scholars have placed Jesus's birth as early as 6 BC and some as late as AD 1. As far as the date for Revelation, we understand it is the last book written, but no one knows the exact date. However, this is another study for another time. The first book written is believed to be the book of James in about AD 46. So, the time period between the writings of the New Testament is between AD 46 and AD 70-97. At most we are looking at all the New Testament *writings* being done in about a fifty-year span. However, the four gospels record events happening before the birth of Christ. That means the *content* of the New Testament is all within a hundred years, at most.

There are a total of 27 books and just like the Old Testament, there were many authors who shared in writing these books.:

- There are men who only wrote one book that took on the author's name – **Matthew, Mark, James, Jude**
- Luke, Acts (sometimes referred to as Acts of the Apostles) – **Luke**
- John, 1 John, 2 John, 3 John, Revelation – **John**
- Romans, 1 Corinthians, 2 Corinthians, Galatians, Ephesians, Philippians, Colossians, 1 Thessalonians, 2 Thessalonians, 1 Timothy, 2 Timothy, Titus, Philemon – **Paul**
- 1 Peter, 2 Peter – **Peter**
- Hebrews (The traditional author is often considered to be Paul. However, names like Apollos, Barnabas, Luke, and even Priscilla and Aquila have been mentioned as possible authors) – **Unknown Author**

Also, just like Old Testament, the New Testament was written and collected without chapters and verses. As the books were gathered into one central location, they were arranged into five categories:

1. **History/The Gospels** – Matthew, Mark, Luke, John
2. **History/Acts of the Apostles** – Acts
3. **Paul's Epistles (Letters)** - Romans, 1 Corinthians, 2 Corinthians, Galatians, Ephesians, Philippians, Colossians, 1 Thessalonians, 2 Thessalonians, 1 Timothy, 2 Timothy, Titus, Philemon
4. **General Epistles (Letters)** – Hebrews, James, 1 Peter, 2 Peter, 1 John, 2 John, 3 John, Jude
5. **Prophecy** – Revelation

# Understanding the Bible

We will look at the overall content of these books in a later chapter, but by arranging the books in this order, it allowed earlier readers to look certain portions of a book up faster by knowing where is was located in each category. I also believe it's important to know what an "epistle" is. This is not a word we use today unless we are talking about the epistles in the Bible. The word "epistle" simply means "letter."

All of Paul's writings are in a letter format. Some of his letters are written to a group of people at a local church (Romans, Corinthians, Galatians, etc.) and some of his letters were written to individuals (Timothy, Titus, Philemon). The General Epistles can be looked at the same way, however, they took on the name of the author of the letter and not the ones receiving the letter. The only exception is the book of Hebrews which is classified as a General Epistle but has taken the name of the group of people to whom it was addressed.

## UNDERSTANDING THE BASICS

There is definitely much more we can say about the breakdown of the Bible. However, this should serve as a good understanding of the basics. If you can know and understand the basic breakdown of the Scriptures, it will help you tremendously in future studies.

The moment I understood *why* the Bible was arranged the way it is, is the moment I started to understand the big picture of the Bible. This is not just a bunch of random books, written by random people, thrown together for a random purpose. God doesn't work in the business of random. Instead, it is a God inspired set of writings that tell the story of God's people from the beginning of time to this very day. Understanding this is something that will help you through your whole spiritual life. God had a purpose. He had a plan. He has a plan for you. What's that plan? Let's find out.

## Chapter 4 Study Questions

1.  What is the difference in knowing and understanding?

2.  Why is this important when it comes to the Bible?

3.  Read 2 Timothy 2:15. What are three things we need to understand about this passage?

4.  What does the word "testament" mean? Why is this important to understand?

5.  What's the difference between Major and Minor Prophets?

6.  What's an epistle? What are the different kinds of epistles we see in the Bible?

7.  Memorize each of the five categories in the Old and New Testaments. After memorizing the categories, write them across the top of a piece of paper. Now see how many books you can list in each category.

8.  Why is it so important to understand the "why" behind the breakdown of the Bible?

# CHAPTER 5
# Two Testaments, One Message

Growing up in a small conservative church, I felt like I had a pretty good grasp on the breakdown of the Bible. I remember having charts up in my classrooms at church that listed all the books of the Bible and the categories in which they belonged. I grew up learning the Bible stories and I also knew the book where the stories could be found. When I got into the middle school and high school classes, there was less emphasis on Bible stories and more emphasis on "teenager issues" like drinking, drugs, sexual immorality, etc. We would look at verses in the Bible that said we shouldn't do those things, be reminded we shouldn't give into peer pressure, and then we were sent back to school on Monday to practice what we had just been taught.

I'm not taking anything away from teaching those principles to teenagers. In fact, where I'm preaching, we are teaching those same things. However, I always felt like there was a major flaw in how I was taught as a young Christian: no one ever explained the *why* behind the Bible stories. Why did I spend all those years learning about Abraham, Isaac, Jacob, Moses, David, Peter, and Paul? Why learn the breakdown of the Bible? All those years seemed pointless to me if all that would happen when I reached middle school and high school is never mention those stories and characters again and we start talking about "important" teenage issues.

Again, I don't want to take anything away from those teenage years and what I learned in those Bible classes. I learned a lot of valuable information, but I always felt like we had crossed a bridge from elementary Bible principles into the advanced spiritual topics. Except I felt like there was no bridge at all. We just jumped headfirst into the deep end.

The summer after my junior year of college, I had the opportunity to participate in my first preaching internship. That summer is when I finally had the time and resources to really begin studying the Bible in depth. Yes, I was at a Bible college, but I was studying what my classes had me study and there really wasn't time leftover for much personal study. But that summer in Danville, KY, I finally found the bridge that explained the *why* behind all those years of Bible study.

## TWO ACTS, ONE PLAY

Understanding the breakdown of the Bible is one thing. Understanding what all sixty-six books of the Bible have to do with one another is a completely different obstacle. Remember the story of the castle? God (the architect) has given us (the builders) the Bible (the blueprint). Remember, architects make blueprints very specific. They tell us exactly where they want windows, doors, and walls. It's our job to look at the blueprint, analyze the blueprint, and use the blueprint accurately. And we are not just looking at the individual components of the blueprint, but the overall picture. Why is the Bible arranged the way it is? Why are the stories in the Bible so important? What's the big picture?

God is not a god of randomness, disorder, and confusion (1 Cor. 14:33), but He is a God of purpose. So, what is the purpose of the Bible? Why does this book mean so much to so many different people? And most importantly, what does the Bible mean to you and me?

I once heard someone say, "the Bible is like a play: there are two acts, but only one play." In a stage production, there is typically an intermission between two separate acts. The acts are usually very different in tone and purpose, but still part of the same play. The first act sets up characters, relationships, and is often light and fun. The first act often ends with a cliff hanger to get you back in your seat after intermission. After intermission, the second act cuts right to the action and purpose of the play. The plot thickens, the climax is reached, and a solution is given. The Bible is very similar. We've already established the two most common sections of the Bible, the Old Testament and New Testament. However, to help us better understand the content and purpose of these two "acts," we must dig deeper.

## THREE TIME PERIODS OF THE BIBLE

As you read through your Bible, you will notice that the tone, surroundings, language, and ideals begin to change. This is due to the fact that from the time the first book (Job) was written to the time the last book (Revelation) was written, is a period of *at least* 1500-1600 years. I believe this is important to the overall message of the Bible. If

# Two Testaments, One Message

Jesus was the answer to sin, why didn't God just bring Jesus from the very beginning? Why did Jesus wait until the New Testament? If this was all about Jesus, what's the point of the Old Testament? Why did so much time go by? These are all questions that have been asked by skeptics of the Bible and I think all these questions deserve answers.

Bible scholars notice three major time periods in the Bible. We are not talking about secular time periods like the "Ice Age" or the "Iron Age," but Biblical time periods. These Biblical time periods are called the Patriarchal Age, Mosaic Age, and the Christian Age. All three of these time periods have different laws, different distinctions, and different purposes in the big picture of the Bible. Understanding these time periods is vitally important to answering questions about the purpose of the Bible.

### Patriarchal Age

The word "patriarch" comes from the Greek word *patriarkhes* which means "chief or head of a family." We seldom use this word today, but every once in a while, you may hear it used to describe the oldest remaining male in a family. He is the patriarch, or the head of the family, that is still living. Once the oldest male dies, the role of patriarch is then given to his oldest son. Again, this holds no significance or meaning in our culture today, but it meant *everything* to the Biblical culture.

The Patriarchal time period is the smallest portion of the Bible, but that does not mean it's any less important than the other two. Most people will place this time period from the beginning of time in Genesis chapter one and it ends with the giving of the Law of Moses on Mount Sinai. So, this means anything you read in Genesis and even the first several chapters in Exodus are included in the Patriarchal time period. Don't forget that Job is even considered to be dated within this time period as well.

There are many key characteristics of the Patriarchal Age that can help you understand your Bible reading and stories a little bit better. First, the characters we see in this time period did not have a written law by which they lived. However, this does not mean they didn't have rules and guidelines.

A second characteristic of the Patriarchal Age is that God spoke directly to the patriarch of the family. Hebrews 1:1 says, "God, who at various times and in various ways spoke in time past to the fathers by the prophets" (NKJV). Throughout Genesis (and even into Exodus with

Moses), we see God speaking directly to the patriarch of the family. We see it first with Adam, then his sons, then through all the generations (see Gen. 5). Eventually God spoke to a descendent of Adam by the name of Abraham. As you keep reading through Genesis, you see that God remains with the same family. After Abraham, God spoke to his son, Isaac. After Isaac, God spoke to his son, Jacob. Jacob actually stole the patriarchal duties from his older brother, Esau (see Gen. 25:29-34). From Jacob, we follow his son, Joseph, and eventually, as years pass between the books of Genesis and Exodus, we see God speak directly to Moses.

Although God's people in this time period didn't have a written law, they did have some sort of rules and guidelines that by which they lived. Because God spoke to His people directly, they knew what was expected of them. God told Adam and Eve not to eat the fruit (Gen. 2:17). Cain and Abel knew about offering sacrifices to God (Gen. 4). When God expected something from His people, He spoke to them. I would suggest that just because they did not have a *written* law, that does not mean they didn't have a *moral* law.

Where there is sin, there is a law declaring what sin is. We know that there was sin in the Patriarchal Age (see Job 1:22; 2:10). God even warned Cain before he killed Abel that "sin lies at the door" (Gen. 4:7).

Where there is sin, atonement needs to be made. Atonement is when there are reparations for doing something wrong. Even if there was no law, there was an understanding that sacrifices needed to be made to God. Other forms of sacrifices we see are thanksgiving, praise or honor, and covenant sacrifices.  We see a long list of sacrifices under the patriarchs:

- Cain and Abel – Genesis 4:1-5
- Noah after the flood – Genesis 8:20-21
- Abraham builds an altar – Genesis 12:1-7
- Abraham almost sacrifices Isaac – Genesis 22
- Isaac builds an altar – Genesis 26:23-25
- Jacob builds an altar – Genesis 35:5-7

Sacrifices played a key role during this time period. Something we will also look at closely in the Mosaic period.

Another characteristic of this time period that I believe is important to understand is that animals were the main gauge of a person's of wealth. The amount of livestock and servants you had in your house is

# Two Testaments, One Message

what determined your place in society. Listen to how Job is described in Job 1:3, "Also, his possessions were seven thousand sheep, three thousand camels, five hundred yoke of oxen, five hundred female donkeys, and a very large household, so that this man was the greatest of all the people of the East." He was the greatest of all the people of the East because of his possessions of livestock and the size of his household.

When offering sacrifices, it had to be an animal. And not just any animal, but your best animal. If animals were your wealth and your livelihood, but you had to sacrifice animals to God, how easy do you think it was to give God the best of your wealth? This is what God expected out of His people. He wanted their best. He wanted to see that they valued obedience to Him more than the wealth of this world.

What we start to see in the opening pages of the Bible, is a standard that was set in place by God. We start to see the big picture come into focus. We see sin enter into the world through Adam and Eve. They didn't obey God's command not to eat the fruit. Because sin entered the world, something would need to make atonement, or fix the wrong of sin. This is where Jesus comes into the picture.

So many people ask, "If Jesus is the main purpose of the Bible, why don't we see Him until the New Testament? Does that mean the Old Testament is all just a waste of time?" These questions come from someone who truly doesn't understand the message of the Bible. From the very beginning, once sin entered the world, God had a plan. Notice what He says in Genesis 3:15, "And I will put enmity between you and the woman, and between your seed and her Seed; He shall bruise your head, and you shall bruise His heel."

This is a direct reference to Jesus Christ. It was Satan that tempted Adam and Eve to sin. Although, Adam and Eve were the ones that sinned (and were punished for their sin), it was Satan who really needed to be punished. God said it would be the "Seed" of the woman who would bruise the head of Satan. Notice the s is capitalized in the word "Seed." This means the translators believe it is talking about Deity. This is Jesus.

Jesus doesn't just show up out of nowhere in the New Testament. We know from John 1 that "In the beginning was the Word, and the Word was with God, and the Word was God. He was in the beginning with God" (v. 1). That Word became flesh (John 1:14). This was Jesus.

Jesus would be the sacrifice to forgive our sins once and for all. The Patriarchal Age is just the foundation of the blueprint. It was a time when God was teaching His children about obedience and sacrifice. What if Jesus had come right away? What if Jesus was put on the cross right after Adam and Eve sinned? Well, His sacrifice wouldn't have meant anything. It would have just been a man hanging on a cross. No significance. No meaning.

Because God loves His people, He set His plan in motion by teaching the importance of sacrifice and obedience. Every story during the Patriarchal Age can be centered around those themes. When love, obedience, and sacrifice were followed, salvation can be seen. There are probably hundreds of themes we can pull from the Bible, but I believe four are at the heart of them all: love, obedience, sacrifice, and salvation.

It's also during this time period that we have a very important covenant (testament or promise) made with Abraham. In Genesis 12 and 15 we see God make three promises to Abraham:

1. **The Promise of Land** (Gen. 12:1). This would become known as the Promised Land or Canaan. Today, this is the area of modern Israel and Jordan on the eastern shore of the Mediterranean Sea.

2. **The Promise of a Nation** (Gen. 12:2). Up until this point, Abraham and his wife, Sarah, could not have children. God promised that his family would become a great nation. We know them as the children of Israel.

3. **The Promise of a Seed** (Gen. 12:3). Abraham is told that through him, all the families of the earth will be blessed. Again, this is a direct allusion to Jesus. Through Abraham's "seed," will come the Savior of the world.

These three promises made during this time period are what drives the story of the Bible forward. Because of Abraham's love, obedience, and sacrifice to God, the entire world would receive salvation. The four themes of the Bible: love, obedience, sacrifice, and salvation are all at the root of God's plan. God always delivered His people from sin and trials. This is even more evident in the next time period.

# Two Testaments, One Message

### Mosaic Age

At the very end of the book of Genesis, the children of Israel are left in the land of Egypt. The story picks up at the beginning of Exodus several hundred years later. We see that the Pharaoh of Egypt became afraid of the growing number of Israelites and feared for the safety of his country. He enslaved the children of Israel and they remained that way for four hundred years.

Moses is the one that God chose to lead His people out of slavery and into the Promised Land. After their release from captivity, Moses leads the children of Israel to Mount Sinai. It was on Mount Sinai where Moses received the Law from God. Most people refer to the Ten Commandments (Exod. 20:2-17) as the Law of Moses. However, the Law is a little bit more than ten "Thou shall not. . . " sayings. In fact, as you read through much of Exodus, Leviticus, and Numbers you receive more and more pieces of the Law. Because the law was given to Moses, it has become known as the Law of Moses (cf. Josh. 8:31; 1 Kings 2:3; Luke 24:44; Acts 28:23). It is from this law that this time period gets its name.

This is the largest portion in our Bibles. It's the Law of Moses that governs the people from Mount Sinai all the way through the death of Jesus on the cross. This means that all the books from Exodus through the end of the Old Testament are under the Mosaic Age. They all were following the Law of Moses. Even into the New Testament, most of Matthew, Mark, Luke, and John describe events are under the Mosaic Law. It wasn't until Jesus died on the cross that the Old Law was done away with. We will have more to say on that in the next section.

The Law of Moses is where we get the term "Old Testament" from. It was within this law that God again promised His people, if they would continue to love, obey, and sacrifice to Him, He would continue to take care of them and save them from their enemies. God said, "in that I command you today to love the LORD your God, to walk in His ways, and to keep His commandments, His statutes, and His judgments, that you may live and multiply; and the LORD your God will bless you in the land which you go to possess" (Deut. 30:16). God continued to set His standard for holy living.

This was God's covenant and promise with His people. It was this law and testament that the judges, kings, and prophets followed. People like Joshua, Samson, David, Solomon, Esther, Ezra, Nehemiah, Daniel, Ezekiel, and Isaiah all lived under the Law of Moses. As we just read in our verse above, if they loved the Lord, walked in His ways, kept His commandments, statutes, and judgments (obedience), then God would bless them (salvation).

Sacrifices continued to be a main characteristic of the Mosaic Age. However, unlike the Patriarchal period, the Mosaic Age had written rules and reasons for all these sacrifices. Leviticus 1-7 is a tedious read, but it helps us to understand the types of sacrifices and the reasons for them. Below is a list and brief description of each sacrifice.

1. **Burnt Offering**—an animal was consumed on the altar with fire. This would atone for the worshipper's sin.

2. **Grain Offering**—grain, flour, and oil were burnt to show gratitude to God. It was a way to show thanksgiving to God.

3. **Peace Offering**—this was an optional sacrifice, often coupled with the burnt offering. This could be for multiple reasons (thanksgiving, giving back to the Lord, or when taking a vow).

4. **Sin Offering**—this dealt with forgiveness from unintentional sins, but it also dealt with ceremonial uncleanness. If you were deemed "unclean" based on the Law of Moses, a sin (sometimes translated as "purification") offering would be made on your behalf.

5. **Guilt Offering**—this not only would offer forgiveness of sins, but you would also give extra as reparation for your wrong doing.

*\*\*There is much more that can be said on the different sacrifices, but this gives you a basic understanding.*

In sacrifices where an animal was offered, there were certain stipulations put in place. The animal had to be "clean." That doesn't mean it needed a bath before being sacrificed, but it needed to be approved and perfect. Not just any animal could be sacrificed, it had to be a certain kind (sheep, goat, heifer, dove, etc.). It had to be spotless and perfect. There were also certain animals that were deemed unclean: pigs, camels, shellfish etc. (Lev. 11; Deut. 14). These were not to be sacrificed or eaten.

# Two Testaments, One Message

God deserves our best. When it came to the sacrifices, God wanted the best. In the book of Malachi, we see that instead of offering the perfect and spotless sacrifices, they were offering animals that were blind, lame, or diseased (Mal. 1:8). The point of a sacrifice is to give up something meaningful. If the animal you are offering didn't mean anything to you, then what good was your sacrifice? God wanted the perfect, spotless, and clean animals to be sacrificed to Him.

Another major component of the Mosaic Age was temple worship. Starting in Exodus 25-26, you see instructions given to build the tabernacle. The tabernacle was a tent where the worship of God would take place. It was a big tent that was easily broken down for travel during the wandering days of Moses. It was separated into two rooms: the Holy Place and the Most Holy Place. The two rooms were separated by a huge veil (or curtain).

The Ark of the Covenant was kept in the very back of the tabernacle in the Most Holy Place. The Ark of the Covenant is what held the Ten Commandments as well as a jar of manna (the food God provided to the Israelites) and Aaron's staff. On top of the Ark, were two cherubim facing each other. This was known as the "mercy seat" (Exod. 25:22). This is where God would dwell among His people. Whenever the tabernacle was set up and the Ark of the Covenant was put in the Most Holy Place, God would descend and fill the tabernacle with His glory.

The priests were the only ones allowed in tabernacle. They were also the only ones allowed to offer sacrifices. When you wanted to worship God and offer a sacrifice, it would be done at the tabernacle with the assistance of a priest. This is where God was, so you were literally bringing your sacrifice to the presence of God.

It wasn't until King David in 2 Samuel 7, when the idea of a temple came to be. David saw that, as king, he was living in a pretty fancy house, but God was still dwelling in a tent (tabernacle). David started to plan and gather material to build a temple and a permanent dwelling place for God. His son, King Solomon, would be the one who actually built the temple. In 1 Kings 8, we have an amazing scene when the temple is completed, and the glory of the Lord filled the temple. God would dwell among His people in the temple. There was a time coming when God would literally live among His people. Jesus would come and live on earth and be with His people.

# Finding My Faith

However, the questions remain, "why not send Jesus sooner?" "Why have a Law of Moses when you could have just sent Jesus?" "Why wait so long?" "What's the point of the Old Covenant if God was just going to bring a "new" one?" Again, what we see is a precedence being set. God was teaching His people about love, obedience, and sacrifice. When those things were followed, God blessed His people (salvation).

When the time came, God sent His Son. Jesus Christ embodied everything that had already been taught in the Scriptures. Paul called Jesus the "chief cornerstone" (Eph. 2:20). The foundation of the blueprint was being built for hundreds of years. The whole time, Jesus was the centerpiece of that foundation. Not one stone was laid without getting us closer to the need of our Savior.

When Jesus finally came, it was not meaningless. Instead, it was the fulfillment of everything that had already been done. Jesus would lead us into something new. He would show us what true love, sacrifice, and obedience were all about. Because He lived each one of those attributes, He offered us a salvation that no sheep or goat could have ever offered us.

### Christian Age

When Christ was born in Bethlehem, He and His parents were still under the Law of Moses. This is evident when we see that Mary and Joseph were following the circumcision and purification laws as well as when His family took a yearly trip to Jerusalem for the Passover (see Exod. 23:14-17 and Luke 2). Jesus lived His entire life under the Law of Moses.

It wasn't until His death on the cross that the Old Law of Moses was done away with and something new was put in place. Jeremiah prophesied about this in Jeremiah 31 when He said, "Behold the days are coming, says the Lord, when I will make a new covenant with the house of Israel and with the house of Judah" (v. 31). Christ is the One who brought the New Covenant. Over the next couple of chapters, we will discuss the reasons why a new covenant was needed and the importance of Christ's sacrifice, but for the time being, let's stay focused on this specific time period.

When we read our "New Testament" in the Bible, remember that the Gospels (Matthew, Mark, Luke, and John) all describe events still within in the Mosaic Age. They cover the life and teachings of Christ from four different perspectives. Each gospel account gives us the detailed death, burial, and resurrection of Christ.

# Two Testaments, One Message

The moment Christ dies on the cross, a few things happen. First, the Mosaic Law is done away with. This is portrayed in several different ways in the New Testament. A few references are:

1. ***The temple veil was torn in two from top to bottom*** (Matt. 27:50-51). This signifies that the one thing (the veil between the Holy Place and the Most Holy Place) separating God and man is now removed. God, in the form of Jesus had come to be with man.

2. ***Temple worship, sacrifices, and priests were now obsolete*** (Heb. 9:11-12) tells us that Jesus didn't use the blood of bulls and goats, but He used His own blood to enter the Most Holy Place "once for all."

3. ***Peter's dream of animals***. In Acts 10-11, Peter has a strange dream. In it, he sees a sheet descending from heaven. In the sheet is every kind of animal. Clean and unclean animals were all together. A voice said, "Get up, Peter. Kill and eat" (Acts 10:13). This signifies that the Old Law that stated certain things were unclean to eat is now done away with.

Now that the Old Covenant had been done away with, the New Covenant took effect. This is the time period that you and I live in today. In the Patriarchal Age, promises were made to Abraham that he would have a great land, a great nation, and a great seed. All three of those came to be during the Mosaic Age in the form of Moses leading the children of Israel to Promised Land of Canaan. However, in the New Covenant and Age, those promises are fulfilled as well. The great Seed came in the form of Christ. The great nation is now all those people who follow Christ (Christians), and the great land is waiting for us in Heaven.

**Patriarchal Age - Promises to Abraham:**
>        Great Seed – Great Nation – Great Land

**Mosaic Age - Promises Fulfilled:**
>        Great Seed → Moses
>        Great Nation → Children of Israel
>        Great Land → Promised Land of Canaan

**Christian Age - Promises Fulfilled:**
>        Great Seed → Jesus
>        Great Nation → Christians
>        Great Land → Heaven

# Finding My Faith

We are not following the Law of Moses. We are not sacrificing animals. We are now living under the sacrifice of Christ. Remember those five sacrifices listed in the Mosaic Period? Jesus was the embodiment of them all. He is our Lamb that offered His own blood. It's His sacrifice that brings us into a relationship with God. John said, "For the law was given through Moses; grace and truth came through Jesus Christ" (John 1:17).

In the Old Covenant, forgiveness came from sacrifices to God. The same is true of the New Covenant, but instead of animals, we have the blood of Christ. Notice the Old Testament imagery used to describe Christ's death; "knowing that you were not redeemed with corruptible things, like silver or gold, from your aimless conduct received by tradition from your fathers, but with the precious blood of Christ, as of a lamb without blemish and without spot" (1 Pet. 1:18-19). We have been redeemed by the precious blood of Christ. He was our perfect lamb without blemish or spot.

It was Christ who took the principles from the Patriarchal and Mosaic Ages and showed us what true love, obedience, and sacrifice looks like. Because of Christ's love for God and His people, He remained obedient to God's plan and offered Himself as a sacrifice so that we can have salvation. Now, Jesus asks us to do the same thing. Jesus said, "If anyone desires to come after Me, let him deny himself, and take up his cross daily, and follow Me" (Luke 9:23).

This is where the term "Christian" comes from. The word "Christian" simply means "belonging to or a follower of Christ." Today, those who decide to deny themselves, take up their cross, and follow Christ and His commandments are considered Christians. This doesn't mean we actually crucify ourselves on a cross, but we live the love, obedience, and sacrifice that Christ showed us.

However, this brings up a myriad of questions. Who can be a Christian? What do I have to do to be a Christian? Why did we need a New Testament? What was wrong with the Old? Why do we even keep the Old Testament in our Bibles? All these questions are asked by people every day and rarely do you find someone who can accurately answer them.

The knowledge in these first few chapters is a lot to comprehend. However, I believe when we truly understand the big picture and the

# Two Testaments, One Message

overall message of the Bible, we can really start to build upon our faith. The Bible is more than a series of sixty-six books, but it's a grand story about love, obedience, sacrifice, and salvation. Remember, it's like a play: there may be different acts, with different tones, and different characters, but the message throughout is still the same.

Understanding the breakdown and message of the Bible is crucial for us to truly understand the purpose for living and using God's word. Now that we understand the Bible a little bit better, it's time to turn the attention to ourselves. What comes next is the next step in finding and strengthening your faith.

## Chapter 5 Study Questions

1. Discuss the meaning behind "two acts, one play" and how this is used to describe the Bible.

2. List the three time periods of the Bible? Why are these important for understanding the overall purpose of God's word?

3. After listing all three time periods, list some characteristics of each one. How do these characteristics help us understand the bigger picture of what's going on in Scripture?

4. What are some ideas and themes that are present in all three time periods? Why are these so important to the bigger picture of the Bible?

5. What are the four major themes of the Bible? How are they evident throughout all of Scripture?

# CHAPTER 6
# Why Do We Need a New Testament?

When I was growing up, my brothers and I loved to play video games. I will never forget saving all my birthday and Christmas money so I could buy my very own Playstation. It was the original one and all my friends had it, which naturally meant I needed it too. Not long after I saved my money and bought one, Sony released Playstation 2. Of course, I had to have it. I remember asking my parents if we could buy the new Playstation 2. Their response was something along the lines of, "Didn't you just buy a Playstation? Why do you need another one?" Technically, they were right. I already had one, but the Playstation 2 had better graphics and better games. It had certain things that the original couldn't offer.

When it comes to the Bible, many people look at the Old and New Testaments and wonder the same things: "Wasn't there already a testament (or covenant) between God and His people? Why did they need another one?" One of the most confusing things about our Bibles is the fact that most people don't know the difference between the Old and New Testaments. In the previous chapters we have talked about the difference in the "makeup" and "content" of the two testaments, but what most people have a problem with is the "why" behind the testaments.

In this chapter we are going to focus on two major questions that people ask. The first question is, "What was wrong with the Old Testament?" And second, "Why do we need the New Testament?" If we already had a covenant, why do we need another? Remember as we go throughout this chapter that a testament is a covenant. It's a promise made between God and His people. When we remember that these were promises and covenants, it's easier to see the blueprint of the Bible working throughout the stories and characters. There are many characteristics about the Old and New Testaments that we covered in the previous chapter. If you haven't read that chapter, I advise you do so now. It will make your understanding of these questions and their answers a lot easier.

## WHAT WAS WRONG WITH THE OLD TESTAMENT?

We live in a society that tells us when something is old or broken, we throw it out and get a new one. Is there a hole in your shoe? Throw it out and get a new pair of shoes. Is your computer really slow? It's time for a new computer. Our society also tells us that if something is outdated or a newer model is available, we have to have the newest and best available. There's a reason why Apple comes out with a new iPhone and iPad every year. They make them newer and better. That's why people from all over the world line up to get the newest iPhone or iPad; we want the newest and best things available.

It's only logical to look at the Bible and ask the question, "If there is a New Testament, what was wrong with the Old Testament?" Many scholars and skeptics of the Bible will conclude that the Old Testament was flawed. People will say that if Jesus was God's ultimate plan, then the Old Testament was doomed for failure from the beginning.

Are we supposed to assume that the almighty and all-knowing God who created our entire universe in just six days gave His people a covenant that was flawed and broken? Are we supposed to believe that the God who created man out of a handful of dust and put the stars in the sky gave His people a faulty system of sacrifices and temple worship? Skeptics are quick to argue that God didn't know what He was doing. They want people to think that God messed up and the New Testament was His last-ditch effort to fix what was broken.

If that is the God we serve, what's to say the New Testament isn't broken too? If the Old Testament failed, then certainly the New Testament can too. Why put our faith in a God who set His people up to fail? Does He want me to fail? Why should I follow God knowing that there is a possibility that Christianity is not the answer? If we are telling ourselves that the Old Testament was a failed experiment that was faulty, broken, and defective, then we are treading in some very dangerous waters.

So, what was wrong with the Old Testament? In short; nothing. I believe the Old Testament had two purposes at its time of origination. First, to reestablish the covenant made with Abraham. Remember, God made three promises to Abraham: a great land, a great nation, and a great Seed. God was reestablishing that same covenant with His people on Mount Sinai and the Law of Moses. All the "rules" and "regulations" given about sacrifices, priests, temple worship, clean and unclean animals, etc. were all given so that the people could live pure and holy lives and receive the promises God was making.

Remember, when we make covenants today, we also promise to uphold our end of the deal. If I buy a house, I sign a contract (or covenant) with the bank to say that I will pay back the money. They promise me money and I promise them I will pay the money back. When a couple gets married, they make vows (or promises) to love and care for each other. In each situation, both parties have their end of the bargain to uphold.

This is what God was doing with His people. By giving His covenant to His people, He was essentially saying, "If you *love* Me, *sacrifice* to Me, and remain *obedient* to Me; I will take care of you and offer you *salvation*" (see Deut. 30:16). Remember, these are the four themes in all of Scripture. These are the promises God made to Abraham and they are the same promises He made to the children of Israel.

The second purpose of the Old Testament was to teach the children of Israel about true love, sacrifice, and obedience. How can we really appreciate our salvation if we don't truly understand our responsibilities in the covenant? Paul says in Galatians, "Therefore the law was our tutor to bring us to Christ, that we might be justified by faith" (3:24).

The Hebrew word for "law" comes from a root meaning, "to throw or to shoot (arrows)." In some forms, it can mean "to point, guide, instruct, or teach." That suggests to us that the purpose of a law was to throw, shoot, point, guide, instruct, or teach someone in the right direction. Paul wrote in 2 Timothy, "All Scripture is given by inspiration of God, and is profitable for doctrine, for reproof, for correction, for instruction of righteousness" (3:16, NKJV). For about 1,500 years, the Old Law was teaching God's people about sacrifice and worship. It was teaching God's people what love and obedience really looked like.

Fast forward to Jesus dying on the cross. If Jesus were to die on the cross in the book of Genesis, it wouldn't have meant anything. However, if you grew up watching your best lamb be sacrificed for atonement of your sins, you have a little more appreciation for the Old Law. If you grew up watching daily sacrifices at the temple and watching the blood pour out of the animals so that *you* could be forgiven, it would make you appreciate that animal's sacrifice so you could live.

If you've already been taught or "tutored" in the Old Testament, it wouldn't take you long to recognize the connection between killing a lamb and killing Jesus. Watching the blood pour from Jesus would have been eerily familiar to watching the blood pour from your favorite lamb (especially during Passover when Jesus died).

Instead of looking at the Old Testament as broken, flawed, or defective, we must see that this was just another building block in God's eternal blueprint (Eph. 2:19-22). There was nothing wrong with the Old Testament, however this wasn't God's eternal plan. When the builders are building a structure, we are so interested in what the end result will be. However, before we see the end result, we must first see the foundation being laid, the studs put in place, and the drywall put up. Even though the structure isn't finished being built, we wouldn't say the studs and drywall were a mistake. It's simply the next step in building the blueprint.

The Old Testament was simply the next step in God's blueprint. But it still begs the question, "If there was nothing wrong with the Old Testament, why do we need the New Testament?"

## WHY DO WE NEED THE NEW TESTAMENT?

My parents didn't understand why I needed a Playstation 2, if my original Playstation wasn't broken. This is how we've been trained to think. There's a saying that goes, "If it ain't broke, don't fix it" (I know that's not proper English, but I live in the South; it's how we speak). Something that isn't broken doesn't need fixing. As we've already seen in the section above, there was nothing wrong with the Old Testament, however that doesn't mean it hadn't been broken.

When speaking of the new covenant that He would establish with His people, God said, ". . . I will make a new covenant with the house of Israel and with the house of Judah— not according to the covenant that I made with their fathers in the day that I took them by the hand to lead them out of the land of Egypt, MY COVENANT WHICH THEY BROKE. . . " (Jer. 31:31-32 emphasis mine). No, there was nothing wrong with God's covenant, but it was broken. It was broken by the flawed people with whom the covenant was made.

# Why Do We Need a New Testament?

The Hebrew writer would say, "For if that first covenant had been faultless, then no place would have been sought for a second" (8:7). This leads many people to assume there was something wrong with the Old Covenant. However, if you read the next verse, you will see exactly what the Hebrew writer saw was wrong with the Old Covenant. "Because FINDING FAULT WITH THEM, He says: 'Behold, the days are coming, says the Lord, when I will make a new covenant with THE HOUSE OF ISRAEL AND WITH THE HOUSE OF JUDAH'" (Heb. 8:8 emphasis mine). Where was the fault? It was not that the Old Covenant was flawed or at fault, but it was the house of Israel and Judah that broke the covenant with God time and time again.

Covenants are broken all the time. When covenants are broken, there are consequences. If I don't pay my mortgage to the bank, I have broken the covenant I have with them. When I don't pay, I could have a lien put on my house, I could be kicked out of my house, and eventually my house could go into foreclosure. If you are a student in school, you probably signed a paper at the beginning of the school year stating that you will follow all the rules that your school has put in place. If you break those rules, there are punishments. Suspension and expulsion are always the big ones.

God gave His children a covenant to follow. He gave them a lifestyle to live. If they kept the covenant, God would continue to bless them and protect them. However, Jeremiah tells us they broke the covenant. They didn't listen to and obey God and therefore, there were consequences. Sin always has consequences. Even in the middle of the consequences, God was prophesying through Jeremiah that a new covenant was coming. Jesus was the answer for how to atone for sin.

Jesus was here for a very specific purpose. For hundreds of years, the foundation of the blueprint was being laid. Sacrifices, temple worship, priests, kings, and prophets were all laying a solid foundation for what Christ was about to do. The "Architect" has now come to earth to start building the blueprint. After Peter's great confession that Jesus was the Christ, the Son of the living God, Jesus responds by saying, "You are Peter, and on this rock I will build My church" (Matt. 16:18). Please note that there is nothing special about Peter, but it was Peter's confession about who Christ was that is the foundation upon which the church would be built.

# Finding My Faith

Jesus said in the Sermon on the Mount, "Do not think that I came to destroy the Law or the Prophets. I did not come to destroy but to fulfill" (Matt. 5:17). The Old Testament was not being done away with, it was being fulfilled. To "fulfill" means "to bring to completion." The plan that started so long ago in the Garden of Eden would now be completed.

In the most agonizing and painful scene in all of Scripture, Jesus is hanging on the cross, struggling to stay alive. He had already been mocked, beaten, tortured, and nailed to a cross. He has spent hours hanging there, pushing Himself up on the nails just to get a breath of fresh air. Finally, when His time had come, "He said, 'It is finished.' And bowing His head, He gave up His spirit" (John 19:30).

"It is finished." Why would He say that? What was finished? That statement should bring two things to mind: (1) Jesus had a purpose in coming to earth, and (2) Now that He's finished, what's next?

What was Jesus's purpose in coming to earth? Remember, in the Patriarchal Age, promises were made to Abraham of a great land, great nation, and a great Seed. Galatians 3:16 says, "Now to Abraham and his Seed were the promises made. He does not say, 'And to seeds,' as of many, but as of one, 'And to your Seed,' who is Christ."

Jesus was the Seed. He was the one through the bloodline of Abraham who would bless all the families of this earth. Through Jesus, all people can become part of the family of God. Paul told us, "if you are Christ's, then you are Abraham's seed, and heirs according to the promise" (Gal. 3:29). Jesus offers us a great land. No, this is not the Promised Land in the Old Testament, but the promised land of Heaven. Jesus did not destroy the Law but fulfilled it. He brought the fulfillment of God's promises to Abraham.

Jesus also fulfilled the Law of Moses by being the ultimate sacrifice for our sins. Remember the sacrifices in the Old Testament? They had to be flawless and clean. Even though Jesus was without sin (flawless), He took our sins to the cross. "For He made Him who knew no sin to be sin for us, that we might become the righteousness of God in Him" (2 Cor. 5:21). Peter even refers to Jesus as "a lamb without blemish and without spot" (1 Pet. 1:19).

As Jesus was predicting His own death, He says, "Now My soul is troubled, what shall I say? 'Father, save Me from this hour'? But for this purpose I came to this hour" (John 12:27). Let's not forget that while on earth, Jesus was a man who could feel pain. He didn't want to go through the horrible death that awaited Him, but He also knew that this was His purpose in coming. His purpose was to die and be our sacrifice. His purpose was to offer His people eternal life and salvation (Rom. 10:13).

"For God so loved the world that He gave His only begotten Son, that whoever believes in Him should not perish but have everlasting life. For God did not send His Son into the world to condemn the world, but that the world through Him might be saved" (John 3:16-17). God and Jesus displayed the most extreme levels of love, obedience, sacrifice, and salvation. It was because God loved the world that He gave His only begotten Son. It was because of Jesus's obedience to God's plan that He went through with the sacrifice on the cross. And it was because of Jesus's obedience and sacrifice that you and I have been offered salvation.

Why do we need the New Testament? The simple answer is because we need Jesus. The Law of Moses was a foreshadowing of the things to come. The Hebrew writer said, "For the law, having a shadow of the good things to come, and not the very image of the things, can never with these same sacrifices, which they offer continually year by year, make those who approach perfect" (10:1). The sacrifices of the animals from the Law of Moses were just an example of what was coming with the blood of Christ. Paul told the Colossian church that the things of the Law were "a shadow of things to come, but the substance is of Christ" (Col. 2:17).

Without Christ, we would still be offering animal sacrifices every time we had sin in our lives. But thanks to Jesus, when we sin, we can go directly to God through prayer (symbolized by the veil torn in two at Jesus's death) and ask Him to forgive us. Leviticus says, "For the life of the flesh is in the blood, and I have given it to you upon the altar to make atonement for your souls; for it is the blood that makes atonement for the soul" (17:11). It is Jesus's blood that atones for our sins and gives us life.

When you take the time to look at the big picture of the Bible, everything starts coming into focus a little easier. Every page in the Bible is a small portion of God's eternal blueprint. Every word of the Bible builds upon the foundation that was laid before it. Hopefully we can now understand the importance of the New Covenant in our lives.

However, even after understanding the necessity for the New Covenant, there are still a few questions that several people ask: "Do we still follow any of the Old Testament? Why is the Old Testament still there? Why keep the Old Testament in our Bibles if it has become obsolete?" When we can understand the answers to these questions, we can truly begin to strengthen the faith within us.

# Why Do We Need a New Testament?

## Chapter 6 Study Questions

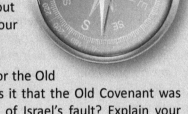

1.  How would you explain the need for the New Testament when there was already a Testament put in place?

2.  What was incomplete about the Old Testament? Explain your answer.

3.  What (or who) was at fault for the Old Covenant being broken? Was it that the Old Covenant was flawed? Was it the children of Israel's fault? Explain your answer.

4.  What was the purpose of the Old Testament at its time of origination?

5.  What was Jesus's purpose for coming to earth?

# CHAPTER 7
# Why Keep the Old Testament in Our Bibles?

There is a story of a farmer who lived a modest life and didn't have many possessions to call his own. He only owned two pairs of overalls. He had a nice pair that he wore to church services and a pair that he wore to work in his fields. When his work pair of overalls would get worn out, he would go and buy a new pair. However, what was once his nice pair of overalls now became his work pair, while the new pair became his new church outfit. And so, the cycle continued.

I do the same thing with tennis shoes. I have two pairs of tennis shoes. One pair for yard work, painting, etc. and a nicer pair to wear out in public. When I get a new pair of tennis shoes, they become my nice pair. I get rid of my old "working" shoes and my once nice pair of shoes becomes my new yard work shoes, and I'm sure this cycle will likely continue this way.

As we stated in the last chapter, our society has been told that when we have something we no longer want or need, it's time to throw it out. According to statisticbrain.com, in 2016, it was estimated that the weekly revenue made from garage sales in the United States was $4.2 million. That is $4.2 million every week that was spent on someone's old furniture and clothes. That means every week people all over our country were getting rid of $4.2 million worth of items they no longer wanted. This is because our society has been told if we no longer need something, it's not worth holding onto.

If we needed the New Testament so badly, why do we still keep the Old Testament in our Bibles? Growing up I always heard that I was a "New Testament Christian." This means that we follow the New Testament and only the New Testament. The doctrines, beliefs, and commands in the New Testament are what shapes my life, while the Old Testament was no longer followed. That seems logical. After all, it's the

# Why Keep the Old Testament in Our Bibles?

"Old" Testament. Of course, it isn't followed anymore. Then why was I still learning all the Old Testament stories in my Bible classes? Why was our preacher still preaching lessons from the Old Testament? If we didn't use it, why did we keep it in our Bibles?

Remember my story from the very first chapter? I was sitting at the computer, watching a debate on homosexuality unfold right before my eyes. The "New Testament Christian" in me was understanding the New Testament arguments against homosexuality. Paul mentioned in Romans that the women were leaving the natural use of a man for other women. The same was true for the men (Rom. 1:26-28). The New Testament says homosexuality wasn't natural. Paul also mentioned in 1 Corinthians 6:9-11 that homosexuals (among other sinners) would not inherit the kingdom of God. For a New Testament Christian, the argument seemed pretty clear.

However, the Old Testament was also being brought up in the argument. The Old Testament states that men should not have sexual relations with other men because it's detestable (Lev. 18:22). I agree with what the Bible says, but just a few chapters later, Leviticus 20:13 says, "If a man lies with a male as he lies with a woman, both of them have committed an abomination. They shall surely be put to death. Their blood shall be upon them."

Critics of the Bible and of Christianity use verses like this one to support their arguments about how Christianity in an intolerable, outdated, and unloving religious group. They will argue that if we believe in the Bible, then we must believe in the *whole* Bible. If we believe in the whole Bible, then we must follow the whole Bible. If we follow the Bible, then why aren't Christians killing homosexuals as Leviticus suggests? Many Christians have been backed into a corner on many "hot button" issues because of this mindset.

Questions like these stem from a lack of understanding of the Bible. This is why the previous chapters are so important. Someone who truly understands their Bible would understand the meaning and significance behind the verses stated above. The Old Law, which includes the book of Leviticus, was done away with once Jesus died on the cross. Leviticus chapter eleven also states we are not allowed to eat shellfish. Yet, I know many Christians who do just that. It's because the Old Law is done away with. We are living under the New Covenant.

So, is it hypocritical to reference the Old Testament during these times of disagreements? What's the role of the Old Testament in a New Testament Christian's life? I believe there are four main reasons why we retain the Old Testament. I understand there are probably dozens of reasons why we still have the Old Testament, however I have experienced four main reasons in my life that have helped my faith grow stronger.

## REASON #1: WE LEARN WHO GOD IS

Who is God? This is a question that has been debated for hundreds of years and thousands of books have been written on the topic. I'm not interested in debating if there is a God and where He came from. There are countless books you can read on those topics. I am assuming if you are reading this book, you already have a strong belief in God's existence. However, we can know someone exists, but not know anything about him or her. There are billions of people who have lived on this earth that believe in God and His existence, but I think very few of those people have taken the time to get to know Him.

I am a huge baseball fan and my favorite team is the Los Angeles Dodgers. My all-time favorite player is Clayton Kershaw. I know he exists because I watch him pitch on TV. I've seen pictures of him and his family on social media. I've never met Clayton, but I know he's real. This is how most people are with God. We see Him all around us and believe in His existence, but we've never taken the time to get to know Him. It's a good start, but if our relationship with God is as extensive as, "I know He exists," then we don't really have a relationship with Him.

Through the pages of the Old Testament, we learn who God is. In the very first verse of the Bible we can learn so much about our God. "In the beginning, God created the heavens and the earth" (Gen. 1:1, NKJV).

- **"In the beginning God . . ."**—God is eternal. He was before time. Our world had a beginning, God was there before the beginning.

- **". . . God created . . ."**—God is the architect. He has the power and knowledge to create matter and life.

- **". . . The heavens and the earth . . ."**—Look around you. Everything you see is made possible because of God. God is the master artist of this beautiful universe.

# Why Keep the Old Testament in Our Bibles?

That's just the first verse of the Old Testament. Can you imagine what you can learn in the other 23,144 verses in the Old Testament? Here are just a few:

- God is merciful, gracious, longsuffering, abounding in goodness and truth (Exod. 34:6-7).
- God is good and upright (Psa. 25:8).
- The Lord is righteous in all of His ways (Psa. 145:17).
- "No one is holy like the Lord" (1 Sam. 2:2).
- God is just (Psa. 99:4).
- God loves His people (Deut. 7:7-8).

Every page we read in the Old Testament is like digging deeper into who God is. John says, "And this is eternal life, that they may know You, the only true God, and Jesus Christ whom You have sent" (17:3). We cannot have eternal life if we do not know God. The Old Testament is there to help us know Him. We are not just going to know *of* Him, but we will actually have a relationship with Him.

When my wife and I were dating, we spent all our time together getting to know each other. Any spare second we had was spent together. We asked questions about our childhood, holidays, family life, likes, dislikes, etc. When we were apart, we wrote letters to each other (cute, I know), talked on the phone, and I'm pretty sure she texted me while she was in her college classes. All Brooke and I wanted to do was talk to each other. The more we talked, the more we got to know each other. The more we got to know each other, the more we liked each other. Soon, that like turned into love. Now we are married and have four children together.

I don't think it's a coincidence that God relates His relationship with His people to our relationships with our spouses (Eph. 5). God speaks to us through His Word, the Bible. The more we read His Word, the more we get to know God. The more we get to know God, the more we like Him. Soon, we learn what love is, because God demonstrated His love for His people countless times in the Old Testament. Every page of the Old Testament teaches us more about God and His love for His people. We learn that by knowing Him, we can have a relationship with Him. And only then will we learn who God truly is.

## REASON #2: WE LEARN ABOUT GOD'S PATTERN

If you are a fan of art, you will notice that all artists has a certain style they will use in all their paintings or drawings. Even musicians have a style of music so that when you hear a certain song, you can almost guess who the singer is before you hear any words. Artists and musicians set patterns or styles for themselves and few deviate from their area of expertise.

God has set a pattern. Remember the illustration of the castle? God is the architect. His blueprint is the pattern that He has followed. The Old Testament shows us that God has not only established a pattern, but He has followed the pattern.

We've already discussed some of these major themes, but consider a few of these patterns that God has created and followed:

1. **God's pattern of love**. Through all the Old Testament stories, we see God's love for His people. He continued to love Adam and Eve even after they sinned. He loved Abraham, Isaac, and Jacob and continued to bless them. He loved Moses and the children of Israel and continued to take care of them in the wilderness and gave them the Promised Land. Even during all the years when kings and the people turned to idols, God continued to love His people. Eventually, it was because "God so loved the world, that He gave His only begotten Son" (John 3:16).

2. **God's pattern of sacrifice**. We just referenced John 3:16. The ultimate sacrifice was Jesus on the cross, but long before that, God was setting a pattern for sacrifice. We know about the sacrifices in the Old Testament and what they meant. These were all pointing toward the sacrifice of Christ. But can you imagine through all those years of animal sacrifices, God knew that it would one day be His Son, Jesus? His pattern was not just that we would sacrifice, but that He would have to give His own sacrifice as well.

3. **God's pattern for obedience**. A lot of people view Christianity as just being obedient to a higher power's list of rules. That couldn't be further from the truth. From the Garden of Eden, God was trying to teach His people about obedience. Adam and Eve were not supposed to eat from

the tree. If God said something, He expected the people to obey and follow through. However, God expected the same thing out of Himself. When God made a promise, He kept it. When God said He would deliver the children of Israel from Egypt, He did it. When He said He would give them the Promised Land, He did it. God said He would send a Savior, and He did it.

4. **God's pattern for salvation**. God was always saving His people. God's love for His people always drove Him to care for and provide for His people. The pages of the Old Testament show us how as they showed love, sacrifice, and obedience toward God, He always took care of His people. However, we also see a pattern being set about what happens when God's people didn't love, sacrifice, and obey Him. Let's just say, it wasn't a pretty picture.

From the pages of the Old Testament, you can get a sense of who God is based on the pattern and blueprint that He established. The more you read the stories of the Old Testament, the more you come to appreciate that God never deviated from His love and devotion toward His people.

## REASON #3: WE LEARN ABOUT GREAT FAITH

In one of the greatest and most popular chapters of the New Testament, we learn about the acts of faith of some of the major "Bible Heroes." Hebrews eleven is often referred to as the "Hall of Faith." In this chapter we read about the great men and women of faith that were able to do wonderful things by remaining obedient to God. The phrase "By faith. . ." is used 19 times.

However, what strikes me about this New Testament passage is the fact that most of the examples of faith are from the Old Testament. "By faith. . .":

- ". . . We understand that the worlds were framed by the word of God. . ." (v. 11; cf. Gen. 1-2).
- ". . . Abel offered to God a more excellent sacrifice. . ." (v. 4; cf. Gen. 4:1-14).
- ". . . Enoch was taken away so that he did not see death. . ." (v. 5; cf. Gen. 5:24).
- ". . . Noah . . . prepared an ark for the saving of His household. . ." (v. 7; cf. Gen. 6-7).

- "... Abraham, when he was tested, offered up Isaac. . ." (v. 17; cf. Gen. 22).
- "... Isaac blessed Jacob and Esau concerning things to come. . ." (v. 20; cf. Gen. 27).
- "... Jacob ... blessed each of the sons of Joseph, and worshiped. . ." (v. 21; cf. Gen. 48).
- "... Joseph ... made mention of the departure of the children of Israel, and gave instructions concerning his bones" (v. 22; cf. Gen. 50:25).
- "... Moses ... was hidden three months ... forsook Egypt ... kept the Passover. . ." (v. 24-28; cf. Exod. 1-12).
- The children of Israel "... passed through the Red Sea. . ." (v. 29; cf. Exod. 14).
- "... The walls of Jericho fell down. . ." (v. 30; cf. Josh. 6).
- "... The harlot Rahab did not perish with those who did not believe. . ." (v. 31; cf. Exod. 2, 6).
- The Hebrew writer said, "time would fail me to tell of. . ." (v. 32) before he mentions more Old Testament characters like Gideon, Barak, Samson, Jephthah, David, and Samuel.
- Still more works were done through faith in verses 33-34. Even "women received their dead raised to life again" (v. 35).

When Paul was writing to the Corinthian church, he brought up the stories of Moses. He talked about some of the good things that happened as well as the bad. He said, "Now these things became our examples, to the intent that we should not lust after evil things as they also lusted" (1 Cor. 10:6). He would later say, "Now all these things happened to them as examples, and THEY WERE WRITTEN FOR OUR ADMONITION. . ." (1 Cor. 10:11 emphasis mine). The things of the Old Testament were written so that we can learn what God expects from His people and the pattern that He has set in place.

The Old Testament is full of stories and testimonies of real people's faith in God. Let's not forget when we read our Bibles that these are real stories about real people. These are not made up. It's not a book of fiction, but of reality. We learn from these stories and know that "by faith" you and I can do amazing things in God's kingdom.

### REASON #4: WE LEARN THE REASON "WHY"

One of the biggest questions about the Old Testament is, "Why?" "Why keep the Old Testament in our Bibles?" "Why have an Old

# Why Keep the Old Testament in Our Bibles?

Testament if it was eventually going to be replaced?" These are valid and fair questions that often go unanswered. However, a closer look into Scripture and we realize that the New Testament writers answered the reason "why."

Remember in the previous chapter we looked at the question, "Why do we need the New Testament?" Look at what the Hebrew writer said, "For the law, having a shadow of the good things to come, and not the very image of the things, can never with these same sacrifices, which they offer continually year by year, make those who approach perfect" (10:1). Paul said the things of the Law were "a shadow of things to come, but the substance is of Christ" (Col. 2:17). The Hebrew writer referred to the Old Testament priests as a "copy and shadow of the heavenly things" (Heb. 8:5). The Old Law was a *shadow* of the good things to come.

When I was a student, we would talk about foreshadowing in my English classes. Foreshadowing is when something happens in a story or novel that is an indicator of something that is coming later. For example, when a character in a story says, "I will go with you as long as you can promise we'll be back before dinner." This is most likely foreshadowing that something will happen to make sure they are not back by dinner. Sometimes you don't know foreshadowing is happening until you read further on in the story.

This is the same thing that takes place in our Bibles. Almost everything we read in the Old Testament is a shadow, or image, of what will happen in the New Testament. Some of the more popular examples of this are:

- **Passover**. In Exodus 12, God instructs His people and the people of Egypt that He would pass over their homes and kill the first-born child unless they spread the blood of lamb on their doorposts. That lamb became a symbol of what saved the firstborn children of Israel. In 1 Corinthians 5:7, we read that "Christ, our Passover, was sacrificed for us." The Old Testament was a shadow of what was coming later.

- **The Tabernacle and Temple.** In Exodus 26, the children of Israel were instructed on how to build the tabernacle. Its purpose was so God could dwell with His people and be worshiped properly. Later, David would give instructions for a permanent dwelling place for God called the temple. In the New Testament, God actually came to earth to dwell with His people in the form of Christ. "In the beginning was the Word, and the Word was with God, and the Word was God . . . And the Word became flesh and dwelt among us . . ." (John 1:1, 14). Later, in John's vision about the new heavens and new earth, he writes, "Behold, the tabernacle of God is with men, and He will dwell with them, and they shall be His people. God Himself will be with them and be their God" (Rev. 21:3). God has always wanted to be with His people.

- **Priests and Sacrifices.** We've already talked about the Old Testament priests and sacrifices in great detail in earlier chapters, they play an integral role in Christ's ministry. Hebrews 4 refers to Jesus as our "great High Priest" who passed through the heaven's "veil" to be with His people. The veil separated God and man. Jesus was with God and passed through the heavens to come be with His people. He then became our sacrifice (Heb. 8-9) just like the offerings from the Old Testament.

- **Noah, the Red Sea, and Naaman.** Three different Old Testament stories all have one thing in common: *water*. Noah was saved in a boat while the flood destroyed the evil and wicked people. The children of Israel passed through the Red Sea safely while the Egyptians were swallowed up. Naaman dipped in the Jordan River seven times and his leprosy was washed away. All three stories illustrate the importance of water during our salvation process. Water was a symbol of one thing being cleansed while getting rid of the impurities. Peter brought up Noah when he wrote, "while the ark was being prepared . . . eight souls, were saved through water. There is also an antitype which now saves us— baptism" (1 Pet. 3:20-21). He used an Old Testament story to illustrate New Testament Salvation. Water saves us— baptism.

All of these Old Testament images were given to us to explain the "why" behind everything in the New Testament. After reading the foreshadowing of the Old Testament, it is easier to see Christ's purpose for His ministry. In both the Old and New Testaments, you see a complete story come to fruition. Without the stories and examples from the Old, we would never truly understand *why* Jesus did what He did.

I think it's interesting that when people want to get rid of their extra junk, they put it on their front lawn and driveways or sell it to other people. Every weekend $4.2 million of junk is sold at garage sales. There's an old saying, "one man's trash is another man's treasure." There are many people who may think the Old Testament is no more than a piece of trash that deserves to be thrown out. It's old, out of date, and we don't follow it. However, I think the Old Testament is a treasure. It's one of the most ancient, yet accurate, pieces of literature our world has. It teaches us who God is, what God expects, and it shows us that a life in service to God is not only possible, but it's the answer to eternity with God.

We have spent the first half of this book going over a lot of information on understanding our Bibles. I realize that we have not touched everything on the topics in these chapters, but my prayer is that we can have a better understanding and appreciation of God's word. I believe understanding and appreciating our Bibles is the first step in finding and strengthening our faith. When we have a firm grasp on God's word, only then can we truly start to live a faith that is strong and durable in the darkness of this world.

Understanding our faith is the first step, using our faith is completely different ball game. Hopefully by now, you are feeling more comfortable with your Bible. Are you ready to take the next step? It's time to find out how to use your Bible to live your faith daily.

## Chapter 7 Study Questions

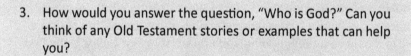

1. Critics often use Old Testament verses to claim there are errors in New Testament Christianity. What do you think about this tactic? Are their flaws in their arguments?

2. List some reasons why we not only keep the Old Testament in our Bibles, but continue to use it.

3. How would you answer the question, "Who is God?" Can you think of any Old Testament stories or examples that can help you?

4. What kinds of patterns has God created and followed?

5. We are left with countless stories from the Old Testament about people's faith and putting their faith in action, what does this mean to you today?

6. Why is it important to understand the "why" behind the Old Testament? How does that help you in your understanding of the New Testament?

# Part Two:
# Using My Faith

# CHAPTER 8
# Using the Bible in My Life

There is a fundamental difference between knowledge and wisdom. We make a grave mistake in thinking those two terms are the same thing. Knowledge is the idea of having facts and information while wisdom is knowing how to use those facts and information.

I got my very first job in high school at a place in our local mall's food court called *Hotdog on a Stick*. For the first week, I had to sit in the back and read through workbooks and answer questions. I read about how to make the lemonade, clean the dishes properly, make the batter for the hotdogs, dip the hotdogs in the batter, and all the other aspects of the job. When I was done with all the booklets, I had to take a test, which I passed. That test stated that I knew what I had read, and I was ready to go up front and begin working. I had the *knowledge*. I knew how to do everything the job required.

A *Hotdog on a Stick* is essentially just a corndog, but we dipped and fried them fresh. Every time a customer ordered a hotdog on a stick, we would take the hotdog, dip it into the batter, and place it in the fryer. I had the knowledge of how to do this from reading all those books and taking the tests, but in all reality, I had no clue what I was doing. I remember dipping my first hotdog in the batter and placing it in the fryer. It was a hot mess! There were clumps of batter falling off the hotdog into the hot oil. When I pulled the hotdog out of the oil, it looked like some sort of swamp monster. Needless to say, I couldn't serve that hotdog. Little did I know, there was a technique on how to dip the hotdog. There was a right way and a wrong way to do it. Once I learned the right way, I was able to do it perfectly almost every time. At first, I had the knowledge, but I didn't have the *wisdom*. I didn't know how to use my knowledge until someone showed me the proper way.

Using our Bible is very similar to this. The first part of this book was about gaining the knowledge about your Bible. But do you have the wisdom to use it properly? Millions of people know their Bibles. Back in

# Using the Bible in My Life

chapter four: *"Understanding the Bible,"* we noted that most Atheists and Agnostics know their Bible better than most Christians, they just lack the wisdom to use it the right way. The Bible is just like any power tool or piece of heavy equipment: use it correctly and it can be very helpful in the job you are doing; use it incorrectly and the consequences could be disastrous, maybe even deadly.

Solomon wrote in Proverbs, "My son, do not forget my law, but let your heart keep my commands; for length of days and long life and peace they will add to you" (3:1-2). He also wrote, "My son, give attention to my words; incline your ear to my sayings. Do not let them depart from your eyes; Keep them in the midst of your heart; For they are life to those who find them, and health to all their flesh" (Prov. 4: 20-22, NKJV). Remember that when we read our Bibles, we are literally reading God's words (2 Tim. 3:16-17). God is the giver of life. When we not only know God's words, but understand and use them properly, wonderful things can begin to happen in our lives.

Now that you have a newfound knowledge of the Bible, how do you use it? I could write volumes of books about how and why to use God's word in your life but let me give you a few things to consider as we continue our journey to find and strengthen our faith.

## ARE YOU HUNGRY?

Have you ever thought about how much we eat in a day? When I wake up, the first thing I want to do is eat my breakfast and drink as much coffee as I can. It's not soon after eating breakfast that I'm thinking about what's for lunch. After lunch I am already thinking about what I'll eat for dinner. Once my kids are put to bed, comes my favorite time of the day: dessert. My wife runs a little "in-home" bakery, so there is always something good for me to have to eat. We eat all day. And when we wake up the next morning, we start all over again.

Our culture runs on food. We eat it all day. We need it to survive, but we also eat it for our pleasure. We see commercials for it on TV and see billboards as we drive down the road. Food is a major part of why and how we survive.

The same was true for the children of Israel. After they were brought out of the land of Egypt, they started to complain because they were hungry and thirsty. I probably would have complained too if I was wandering in the middle of the desert with no food or water.

God listened to His people and provided them with water, quail, and manna. This wasn't just a one-time event. God continued to provide for the children of Israel every day except the Sabbath Day (He gave them enough the day before the Sabbath to last).

Notice what Moses writes about this event in Deuteronomy 8:3. He says, "So He humbled you, allowed you to hunger, and fed you with manna which you did not know nor did your fathers know, that He might make you know that man shall not live by bread alone; but man lives by every word that proceeds from the mouth of the LORD." God was trying to teach the children of Israel a lesson. God wanted them to see that their hunger and thirst would always return, but the words of God are what gave true nourishment and fulfillment.

They needed to learn to trust in God. They needed to learn to listen to Him and know that He would provide and take care of them. Jesus told the woman at the well in John 4, "whoever drinks of this water will thirst again, but whoever drinks of the water that I shall give him will never thirst. But the water that I shall give him will become in him a fountain of water springing up into everlasting life" (John 4:13-14). Again, in John 6, Jesus said, "I am the bread of life. He who comes to Me shall never hunger, and he who believes in Me shall never thirst" (6:35).

No, God is not going to literally feed us and give us water that will never make us hungry or thirsty ever again, but what He offers us is the spiritual nourishment that will lead to eternal satisfaction. It's only in God's word that we can find that nourishment. I don't think it's any coincidence that in the Sermon on the Mount, Jesus says, "Blessed are those who hunger and thirst for righteousness, for they shall be filled" (Matt. 5:6).

So many people are searching for meaning in their lives. So many people are looking for answers to life's hardest questions and circumstances. God has the answers. God's word has the knowledge and will give us the wisdom to answer these questions. The question is, "are you hungry for God's word?" When we are hungry for food, we eat. What are you doing to fulfill your spiritual hunger? Here are some tips and ideas to fulfill your hunger and thirst for righteousness:

1.  Find a local congregation and start attending regularly (see more in chapter 11: "Using the Bible in My Congregation").

2.  If your local congregation offers Bible classes, make sure to attend these as often as possible. You would be surprised by

# Using the Bible in My Life

how many people view these classes as "optional." Why would you want to pass up another opportunity to feast upon God's word?

3. Get involved with teaching classes at your local congregation. The best way to learn God's word is to teach God's word.

4. Get involved with the church members outside of church services. Some congregations offer in-home Bible studies and fellowship. Even spending time with other Christians by going out to meals or inviting someone into your home can help you learn more about God's love and His word.

5. Set aside a certain amount of time each day to read, study, and pray about God's word. I have often found it useful to set an alarm on my phone or computer reminding me to read the Bible.

6. Find an accountability partner like a friend, spouse, or a fellow churchgoer to help you stay on track. Having someone else hold you accountable will help you push each other farther and you will even grow closer together in the process.

If you are hungry and thirsty enough for God's word, you will find time to fulfill that need. However, it's only when we have a steady diet of God's word in our lives that we can truly begin to learn what satisfaction really feels like.

**WATCH YOUR STEP**

Every person we come in contact with is on a journey through this life. Each one of us makes decisions every day that will take us deeper down life's twists and turns. How do we know where we are going? Where do the paths lead?

Jesus told us there are only two paths to take in life. He said, "Enter by the narrow gate; for wide is the gate and broad is the way that leads to destruction, and there are many who go in by it. Because narrow is the gate and difficult is the way which leads to life, and there are few who find it" (Matt. 7:13-14). The broad path is the way of the world. It's the way of sin, selfishness, and pride. The narrow path is the path less taken, but it is the way of righteousness. It's a more difficult path in life because it means humility, selflessness, and obedience.

# Finding My Faith

If I were to survey all the readers of this book, I'm sure we would all choose to take the narrow path. We understand that is the path that leads to eternal life. We understand this is the path Jesus wants us to take. However, many people do not know how to stay on this path. It's narrow and difficult. It's full of hardships and trials. Sometimes it is much easier to take the broad path with everyone else.

I remember going camping when I was younger, and we went on a night hike. We walked along a marked path so we wouldn't get lost, but even then, the path was almost impossible to navigate without some sort of flashlight. At one point in the hike, we turned our flashlights off and we found ourselves hitting tree branches and starting to wander off the path. It was the light that helped us navigate the path in the darkness.

Sometimes we need some help navigating the narrow path of life. The Psalmist says, "Your word is a lamp to my feet and a light to my path" (Psa. 119:105). Notice what helped the Psalmist see where he was going and stay on course: it was God's word. Are you using God's word to light your path? Life is dark and dangerous at times. There are trials and temptations that will pull us off our path. Sometimes it feels like no matter how hard we try to stay on the narrow way, Satan is there to offer a detour. If we have any hope of navigating our way through the trials and hardships of life, it is going to be by not only knowing God's word but using God's word.

In John 8:12, Jesus said, "I am the light of the world. He who follows Me shall not walk in darkness but have the light of life." I think this is a direct reference to Psalm 119:105. If God's word is a lamp to our feet and a light to our path, Jesus is now claiming to be that light. It's no coincidence that John also refers to Jesus as "the Word" (John 1). Jesus, the Word, is the light to our path. We must let the word of God be the guide of our lives.

It's just like a light house guiding a ship through a dark and dangerous storm. As the ship draws close to the dangerous rocks near the shore, it's the lighthouse that guides the ship to safety. Let God's word guide you to safety. This means we will take the necessary time to read, study, and understand God's word. Some future chapters will look at how to let God's word guide you in important decisions. If we let it, God's word will make the narrow path of life into a very manageable and enjoyable journey.

# Using the Bible in My Life

**WALK STRAIGHT**

Have you ever been driving down the road and seen a field of crops? The farmers who plant the fields are remarkable in what they do. The lines of crops are always perfectly straight and perfectly spaced apart. I've always wondered how they get their lines so straight and perfect. If I were in charge of planting, the lines of crops might look similar to a bowl of spaghetti. That's probably why I'm not a farmer.

Paul wrote to Timothy, "Be diligent to present yourself approved to God, a worker who does not need to be ashamed, rightly dividing the word of truth" (2 Tim. 2:15). The term "rightly divide" is actually an old farming term. Just like farmers are careful to plant their crops in neat, perfect, straight lines, we should strive to handle God's word with the same care and attention. It is our responsibility to make sure God's word is being handled accurately. In the verses before and after the one just mentioned, Paul reminds Timothy not to give into strange teachings and stand up against those who try to misinterpret God's word. To "rightly divide" means we will do two things:

1. Know and understand God's word—(part one of this book)

2. Accurately live and teach God's word—(part two of this book)

Again, it's one thing to understand God's word, but to use it properly is a completely different ballgame. Both are vitally important to our spiritual health. Remember the illustration of the castle? God has given us a blueprint to follow. He is the architect and we are the builders. It is our responsibility to make sure we are building the blueprint accurately and responsibly. The moment I deviate from God's blueprint, I have deviated from the architect's plan. It's the same thing as a farmer plowing his crops in crooked lines.

This is also a reminder of the importance of using God's word in our lives. If I drive by an empty field, I often wonder about all of the things that field could be used for. It could be used for crops, homes, businesses, etc. An empty field is useless. Paul wrote, "For we are God's fellow workers; you are God's field, you are God's building" (1 Cor. 3:9). It's time we take the word to the field. The world needs workers to plant the seeds of the Kingdom and build the blueprint of God. It is up to us to rightly divide the word of truth.

Let's not forget what else Paul told Timothy in our above verse. The work of accurately handling and using God's word needs diligence and it's something we should not be ashamed of. Please, never be ashamed of using God's word in your life. If we are going to use God's word in our lives, it should be with boldness and confidence knowing that the word of God is accurate and complete, lacking nothing. Paul said, "For I am not ashamed of the gospel of Christ, for it is the power of God to salvation for everyone who believes. . . ." (Rom. 1:16).

There is power in the word of God and the gospel of Christ. When handled properly, God's word can do wonderful things in your life and in the lives of others.

I think many of the problems we see in religious communities today come from the fact that most people don't know properly how to use God's word in their lives. Sure, they love God and want to do what's right, but very few people actually take the time to make sure God's word is being handled properly. If our faith is going to find strength and maturity, it's going to be by having a steady diet of God's word, using it to light our path, and using it accurately. Only then can we truly begin to gain the knowledge and wisdom needed to succeed spiritually.

As we move forward in the coming chapters, there will be some things that might make you a little uncomfortable. We will ask questions that maybe you've never considered before. I may challenge some beliefs you have had since you were a young child, but please remember that our goal is to use God's word accurately. We don't want to change God's word, but make sure it is being rightly divided. The coming chapters may make you question things you thought you had the answers to, but in order to find *your* faith in God, you have to let God's word tell you what is right and wrong. Don't let your thoughts, feelings, and emotions dictate what is accurate or not.

Are you ready to use God's word to answer the tough questions? Let's take the next step in finding our faith.

## Chapter 8 Study Questions

1.  What is the difference between knowledge and wisdom? Can you think of an example in your life when you had knowledge, but not wisdom?

2.  If you are going to obtain wisdom, why is it important to be hungry and thirsty for God's word?

3.  Listed above are some ways you can fulfill the hunger for God's word. What are some other ways you can feast upon God's word?

4.  We all have trials and temptations in our lives. How have you seen God's word guide you through the darkness?

5.  What are some ways you can make sure you are rightly dividing the word of truth? Why is it so important to make sure God's word is being handled accurately?

# CHAPTER 9
# Building My Spiritual Life

I remember sitting in one of my college classes, listening to one of my professor's lecture about the given topic for that day. As I sat there and stared at the PowerPoint images on the screen, I noticed that my hand was quickly writing down the notes and major points of the lesson. It was almost as if my hand was moving without being told what to do. My hand was writing word for word what was on the slides, but my mind was in a fog and completely blank. I wasn't really paying attention to the teacher and I definitely wasn't paying attention to what I was writing down. After all, it was college and I was probably up late the night before.

Unfortunately, the class I was sitting in was a Bible class. Here I was, listening to God's word being taught, yet I wanted to be anywhere else but in that classroom. I was so privileged to sit and listen to some of the top Biblical scholars in the world, and I found my mind daydreaming about what the cafeteria would have for lunch. Why was I not paying better attention to God's word? Why did I not take it more seriously? People, along with me, were paying good money not only to go to college, but to have the privilege of studying God's word. Yet, I was completely unfocused and uninterested.

Something clicked with me my sophomore year of college: I had built a strong faith in God, but I never built a strong spiritual life to go with it.

## WHAT'S THE DIFFERENCE?

Most people look at their faith and their spiritual life as the same thing. However, I believe they are two completely different things. In earlier chapters, we defined faith as "the assurance of things hoped for and the evidence of things not seen" (Heb. 11:1, NKJV). This is the definition found in Scripture. Faith is essentially just our belief and reliance upon God.

# Building My Spiritual Life

As Christians, our faith is directly related to the belief that there is a God who made this entire universe (Gen. 1). We have faith that God has created an eternal home called heaven (Rev. 21-22). We have faith that God sent His Son, Jesus Christ, to die for our sins, and be resurrected from the dead (1 Cor. 15:1-4). These are truths that we believe in even though we cannot see or experience any of them. We rely on evidence around us to be assured of the things hoped for and things not seen.

A spiritual life is much deeper than just having faith. Someone once said that a spiritual life is "a life that reflects a faith in God." Jesus said in the Sermon on the Mount, "Not everyone who says to Me, 'Lord, Lord,' shall enter the kingdom of heaven, but he who does the will of My Father in heaven. Many will say to Me in that day, 'Lord, Lord, have we not prophesied in Your name, cast out demons in Your name, and done many wonders in Your name?' And then I will declare to them, 'I never knew you; depart from Me, you who practice lawlessness!'" (Matt. 7:21-23).

Does that verse scare you? Jesus said there will be people who believe in Him yet fail to live the right kind of life. They had the faith, but they didn't have the spiritual life to go with it. Sure, they prophesied, cast out demons, and did many wonders in the name of the Lord, but they failed to do the will of the Father. Today we might say, "I believe he is a good, moral person." Or, "she grew up going to church." We might say, "This is a person of faith." Unfortunately, those are not indicators of a strong spiritual life. Jesus put a heavy emphasis on the fact that those who do the will of the Father will be the ones to enter into heaven.

What I found out while sitting in that college class was that I could have all the faith in the world, but if I wasn't living my faith, then what good was my belief in God? Our faith and spiritual lives are very closely connected, but they are not the same thing. I cannot have a spiritual life without my faith in God. However, if all I have is faith in God, but my life doesn't reflect that belief, then I have completely missed the point of Scripture.

**BY FAITH. . .**

How seriously do you take your spiritual life? Most people think that just because they have faith in God, they are doing just fine. I think it's time we take a serious look at the attitudes behind the lives we are living. Up until college, I had a strong faith in God, but never took the time to build my spiritual life. The term "spiritual life" is never found in the Bible, yet it's something that can be seen (or not seen) in almost every character we read about.

Although we've already discussed Hebrews 11 in a previous chapter, I think it's worth taking another look. All these great men and women we read about in the Scriptures all had faith in God. That was the bond that ties them all together. However, it was not their faith in God that made these men and women special. It was their actions and their lives. If you take the time to read Hebrews 11, you will see that it was "By faith . . ." that these people were able to do the wonderful things we read about in Scripture. It was because they believed and trusted in God that they were able to do courageous, heroic, and miraculous things.

A spiritual life is not just a life that believes in God, it is a life that lives for God. Jesus said in John 14:15, "If you love me, keep my commandments." A life of faith should lead us to a life of following, loving, and keeping His commandments. Remember in part one of this book, we looked at how the entirety of Scripture teaches us about love, obedience, sacrifice, and salvation. This is at the heart of our spiritual life. When we love Christ and place our faith in Him, this should lead us to a life of obedience and sacrifice. If we love Him, we will keep His commandments. When those steps of love, obedience, and sacrifice are followed, salvation follows.

## LOOKING INWARD

My guess is you are reading this book because you believe in God. According to a 2014 study by Pew Research Center, 89% of Americans believe in God.[1] If 89% of Americans believe in God, then why is the morality in this country continuing to decline? Why is abortion still legal? Why is same-sex marriage becoming legal? Why is crime continuing to rise when well over the majority of Americans believe in God?

The simple answer is because although people believe in God, they are not living for God. They are not letting their faith lead them to live a healthy spiritual life. People today will confess their belief in God, but if God's word contradicts the lifestyle they want to live, then they just choose not to follow it. Instead, we should be allowing our faith in God and His word to dictate how we act, what we say, where we go and how we treat other people.

Do you remember the incident from chapter one about homosexuality? I know several people who believe in God yet choose to accept homosexuality. How can they do that? If we have faith that God is who the Bible says He is, how can we accept or even practice certain sins that the God we believe in clearly condemns? Sure, the "big" sins like murder and theft are off limits. Unfortunately, we have accepted the "little" sins into our lives and claim that they are "normal" or "not a big deal." Gossip, slander, lying, cursing, flirting with someone who isn't your spouse, inappropriate internet activity, and selfishness have all slowly made their way into the lives of Christians.

If I choose to believe in God, then I am choosing to believe that He is the Creator of this universe. I am choosing to accept that He is all-powerful, all-knowing, and the ultimate authority. I am choosing to accept that He is the architect and I am just the builder. If the architect and all-powerful God says something in His word, as the builder, I should not only accept it, but I should live it.

In the book of Romans, Paul addressed this issue head on. He wrote in chapter one, "For since the creation of the world His invisible attributes are clearly seen, being understood by the things that are made, even His eternal power and Godhead, so that they are without excuse, because, although they knew God, they did not glorify Him as God, nor were thankful, but became futile in their thoughts, and their foolish hearts were darkened" (v. 20-21).

From the beginning of time, God can be clearly seen in His creation. Although we cannot see God, we can clearly see the evidence of God (faith). When it comes to knowing there is a God, Paul says we "are without excuse." However, although people know God and can clearly see His attributes in His creation, they did not glorify Him as God, they weren't thankful, their thoughts were futile, and their hearts were darkened. In other words, they knew God, but you would never have known it based on the lives they were living.

"Professing to be wise, they became fools" (Rom. 1:22). They turned to lives of sin and accepted all the vain things this world has to offer (Rom. 1:28-31). And here is the scariest part of what Paul writes: it's not just the people who choose to participate in the sins of the world, but it's also those who *accept those who participate* in them. "Those who practice such things are deserving of death, not only do the same but also approve of those who practice them" (Rom. 1:32).

*Here lies the problem with most people's spiritual life: we all want to accept God as an all-powerful being, but very few people want to accept the lifestyle that comes along with it.* Some people have called this brainwashing. However, we need to understand that if we have *chosen* to believe in God, then it's not brainwashing. If I have *chosen* to believe in God, then I must *choose* to live my life according to His word.

It's time we take a long look inward. Do I let my own wants, thoughts, and desires determine how I feel about God's word or do I let God's word determine my wants, thoughts, and desires? Do I believe in God? Most people do. Do I follow Him? Most people do. . . partially. It's not good enough to just believe in God. We must have such a deep conviction and belief in who God is so that the only logical solution for our lives is to glorify Him as God.

Ask yourself right now, "Do I believe in God?" If you answered yes, good for you. However, answering, "yes" is only half the battle. What are you going to do with your belief in God? You can choose to waste it on the sins and pleasures of this world, or you can invest it in eternal life. That starts with living your life for God.

## BE TRANSFORMED

We cannot begin to build something if we do not know what we are building. I hope by now we understand the importance of not just having faith, but also having a spiritual life. But what does a spiritual life look like. What does God expect from you and me?

First, we need to understand God's love for us. I have heard countless people, especially young people, say they aren't going to give their lives to God because God doesn't care about them. I have heard excuses like, "God doesn't want me," or "God couldn't forgive me for what I've done," and even, "God only loves those who love Him." These statements and other excuses like them couldn't be more false. These people choose not to follow God because they feel like God doesn't want them or they are unworthy to follow God.

Let's be clear: God wants you. God wants you to love Him. God wants you to spend eternity in heaven with Him. God wants you and loves you. One of the most popular verses in all the Bible is often the most forgotten: "For God so loved the world that He gave His only begotten Son, that whoever believes in Him should not perish but have everlasting life" (John 3:16). He's talking about you and me. God loved us enough to send His Son to die for us. And yes, we weren't worthy enough for an honor like that. You and I have sinned and fallen short of the glory of God (Rom. 6:23). "But God demonstrates His own love toward us, in that while we were still sinners, Christ died for us" (Rom. 5:8). We have to understand God loves us and wants to spend eternity with us.

Second, we have to understand God's will for our lives. Remember who Jesus said would inherit the kingdom of heaven? "He who does the will of My Father in heaven" (Matt. 7:21). So, what is the will of God? Paul writes, "I beseech you therefore, brethren, by the mercies of God, that you present your bodies a living sacrifice, holy, acceptable to God, which is your reasonable service. And do not be conformed to this world, but be transformed by the renewing of your mind, that you may prove what is that good and acceptable and PERFECT WILL OF GOD" (Rom. 12:1-2, emphasis mine).

Do you remember the sacrifices from the Old Testament? Paul tells us that our lives should resemble those sacrifices. Instead of blood and death, he says we should be a *living* sacrifice, holy, acceptable to God. Jesus took care of the blood and death part. If we truly believe that Jesus rose from the dead, then our lives should mimic the same sacrifice. We should die to the sins of the world and start living a new life in service to God (Rom. 6).

When we die with Christ through baptism, a transformation takes place. Our minds should be renewed. Paul tells us in the above verses that in order to live our spiritual lives, we must not be conformed to the world, but be transformed by the renewing of our minds.

To be conformed to something means to comply or be similar in form. I think of Playdough. My sons love Playdough. We will go get some of my wife's cookie cutters and make all different kinds of shapes with their Playdough. If we are using a heart shaped cookie cutter, guess what shape will be made in the Playdough? A heart. If we are using a star shaped cookie cutter, we can expect a star to come out of the Playdough. That's conforming. The Playdough is being conformed to whatever shape the cookie cutter says it should be. Unfortunately, this is what we allow the world to do to us. Yes, we might believe in God, but we allow the world to shape us, mold us, and conform us into how it thinks we ought to look.

Instead, Paul says we should be transformed. When something is transformed, it makes a dramatic change in appearance. My favorite thing to do with Playdough is make pizza. I roll out the dough, use white Playdough for the cheese, some red Playdough for the pepperoni, etc. I don't use cookie cutters, instead I transform the dough into what I want it to be.

When we transform our minds, it means we will completely change our way of thinking and the lives we live. If we simply believe in God, but we haven't changed our behavior. . . what good have we really done? Notice the attributes Paul lists in Romans 12 of a transformed life:

- Love one another (v. 9-10)
- Abhor or hate evil (v. 9)
- Be diligent or consistent (v. 11)
- Be fervent or passionate in Spirit (v. 11)
- Rejoice in hope (v. 12)
- Be patient in tribulation (v. 12)
- Be steadfast in prayer (v. 12)
- Be hospitable towards people we love and strangers (v. 13)
- Be unified to the body (v. 15-16)
- Be humble (v. 16)
- Do good and don't repay evil for evil (v. 14, 17-21)

Unfortunately, so many people go through their lives believing in God, but never make any changes to their lives to reflect their faith. Don't be conformed to the world. It's time we transform ourselves into who God wants us to be. There have been too many people who claim to love God and serve Him, but don't follow God's blueprint for their lives. This has led to a lot of confusion in the religious world. How can we all believe in the same God, but act so differently? How can we all read the same book, but believe different things? It's time we start appreciating God's word as the authority in our lives. It's time we start letting our faith carry us into a closer relationship with God and His Son.

Most people who live a spiritual life for God call themselves Christians. Am I a Christian just because I have faith in God? Am I a Christian just because I try to live a good life? Are all "Christians" created equal?

## Chapter 9 Study Questions

1. What is the difference between having faith and living a spiritual life?

2. What is the ultimate problem with people's spiritual lives?

3. If we are going to build our spiritual lives, what two things do we have to understand? Why?

4. What does it mean to be a living sacrifice?

5. What's the difference between conform and transform? Explain the differences in our spiritual lives.

# CHAPTER 10
# Are All "Christians" Created Equal?

I am married to one of the best cooks and bakers in the world. I have never had a bad meal from my wife and I especially have never had a bad tasting dessert. I try to eat some of her desserts every night after our boys are in bed. I don't play favorites with desserts and I don't discriminate. Cakes, pies, cookies, brownies, . . . I will eat it all. I will even occasionally help my wife in the kitchen with the cooking and baking.

I have learned that while baking, it is extremely important to follow the recipe. The ingredients and their amounts are carefully measured and documented so you know exactly when to add it and how much to add. If you're making chocolate chip cookies and you decide to add pecans instead of chocolate chips, you won't get the desired product. Add too much salt and the cookies will be inedible. Or what if you run out of flour and decide to substitute some extra sugar? You get the idea.

Recipes are very exact for a specific purpose. If you want the desired product, you are going to follow the recipe. When you start adding and taking away ingredients, that's when things get a little out of control. I hope this sounds familiar to you because this is exactly what we talked about in chapter 3: "Building a Castle." If you need to, it might be a good idea to reread that chapter before continuing on.

We've already established earlier in this book that 89% of Americans consider themselves Christians and there are over 43,000 different types of churches who consider themselves "Christian." It's not unusual to drive through any town and see Methodists, Calvinists, Baptists, Pentecostals, Disciples of God, Church of God, Disciples of Christ, and Church of Christ, just to name a few. Even within all those names, you can find words added like United, Primitive, or First United to break them down even further. This does not include non-denominational groups, community churches, and mega churches that have no affiliation with any certain groups. We should note: some of the churches mentioned above consider themselves non-denominational. Yet, all of these churches claim to be Christians and claim to follow the teachings in the Bible.

The realm of churches who consider themselves "Christian" has become a confusing maze of denominations, self-started churches, and long-lasting traditional names to which they hold fast. They all claim to be going to heaven and they all claim to have the right answers. They all claim to get those answers from the Bible. This led me to ask some questions. How can everyone be right? How can we have 43,000 different types of churches who all consider themselves "Christian" if we all believe the same thing and want to end up in heaven? Are all "Christians" equal? Does it matter where you worship, what you believe in, or what you follow as long as you wear the name "Christian?" Can we all take different paths and end up at the same destination?

I noticed something throughout my years of preaching: Christians are like chocolate chip cookies; Jesus gave us a recipe, but somewhere along the way, people have decided to change the ingredients. My goal in this chapter is to go back to the recipe. It's time we look at the blueprint and find our answers. I am not interested in a preacher's answers. I don't care what your preacher, elders, bishops, or parents think . . . and neither should you. We want to find out what *Jesus* thinks.

**WHAT IS A CHRISTIAN?**

The word Christian is first used in Acts 11:26. It says, "And when he had found him, he brought him to Antioch. So it was that for a whole year they assembled with the church and taught a great many people. And the disciples were first called Christians in Antioch" (NKJV). But why were they called Christians? Did they need a cool name for their new club? Were they forming a secret society and needed a way to identify themselves? The answer is actually given just a few verses earlier in Acts 11.

In verses 19-20, we see that men were "preaching the LORD JESUS" (emphasis mine). After they heard the teachings about Jesus, "a great number believed and turned to THE LORD" (v. 21, emphasis mine). Barnabas was sent to these believers and encouraged them to "continue with THE LORD" (v. 23, emphasis mine). As Barnabas taught, "a great many people were added to THE LORD" (v. 24, emphasis mine). It was this group of believers that "were first called Christians in Antioch" (v. 26).

# Finding My Faith

Did you notice what was being taught to the men and women in Antioch? Jesus. Did you notice who the people turned to once they were taught about the Lord? To Jesus. Did you notice who they were encouraged to continue with? Jesus. Did you notice who the believers were added to? Jesus. Do you see the pattern? Do you see the main ingredient in this recipe? It's Jesus.

Jesus is our Lord. He is the Christ and Messiah. In the original Greek language, Christ simply means "anointed one or chosen one." Christ is not Jesus's last name, but His title. Jesus the Anointed One. As the disciples were taught about Jesus, turned to Jesus, continued with Jesus, and added to Jesus, they became followers of Jesus. In fact, Acts 11:26 says, "the DISCIPLES where first called CHRISTIANS . . ." (emphasis mine). A disciple was a student or a follower of a specific teacher. The disciples in Acts were following Jesus.

So, why would they call themselves Christians? The word Christian literally means, "follower of Christ; belonging to Christ." It was a term of dedication and commitment. By calling themselves Christians, they were dedicating their lives to a lifetime of serving and belonging to the anointed Lord.

But all this brings up another interesting question? Can just anyone be added to the Lord? What do I have to do in order to become a Christian?

## ADDED TO THE LORD

In Acts 11, we saw that after being taught about Jesus, the disciples were being added to the Lord (v. 24). I think it's safe to assume that in order to become a Christian (or a follower of Christ), you must be added to Him. But how?

When my wife bakes, she always uses a recipe. There are two sections to a recipe: the ingredients and the step by step instructions. The ingredient list will show every ingredient and their amounts (e.g., 3 eggs, 2 cups of flour, 1 cup of sugar). When you get to the step by step instructions, they tell you how to properly combine all the ingredients to get your great tasting dessert. Have you ever noticed in this section of the recipe; it will rarely tell you how much of the ingredient to add? It might say, "mix together the eggs, flour and sugar until thoroughly combined. . . ." Why doesn't it tell us how many eggs, or how much flour and sugar? It's because it has already told us in the ingredient list. It assumes you've already read and understood the ingredients and how much you will need.

The Bible is the same way. Acts 11 tells us that disciples were being added to the Lord. Why doesn't it tell us how? Well, no, because the ingredients have already been given earlier in the book.

In Acts 2:14-36, Peter gives an amazing sermon about Jesus being God's Son who was sent here to fulfill prophecy and redeem us from our sin. However, the people rejected Jesus and killed Him. But God raised Him up from the dead and sat Jesus on the throne at the right hand of God (Acts 2:30-33). Peter ends his sermon by saying "Therefore let all the house of Israel know assuredly that God has made this Jesus, whom you crucified, both Lord and Christ" (Acts 2:36).

After hearing Peter's message (which I suggest you read in its entirety), the people were cut to the heart (v. 37). They realized they had sinned against God by putting the Lord and Christ on a cross. They had sentenced Him to death because they didn't believe Jesus while He was among them. God's Messiah was beaten, mocked, spit upon, and killed . . . and they were the ones that did it. Realizing their sin, they asked "what shall we do?" (Acts 2:37).

Peter's response is simple, "Repent, and let every one of you be baptized in the name of Jesus Christ for the remission of your sins; and you shall receive the gift of the Holy Spirit" (Acts 2:38). Those are Peter's ingredients for salvation. When we have sinned against God, we need to make it right. How do we do that?

- **Repent.** I call this "a spiritual U-turn." You see your life headed down a dangerous road filled with sin, but you need to fix it. You repent. You turn your life around. You stop living in sin and ask for forgiveness.

- **Be baptized.** Baptism in the Bible is a water baptism by full immersion. What you don't see in the Bible is baptism by sprinkling water on foreheads or babies being baptized. Baptism happened when an individual came to *their own* realization that sin is in their lives and they need Jesus to fix it.

After Peter gave these people the way to salvation, Acts tells us "those who gladly received his word were baptized; and that day about three thousand souls were added to them" (Acts 2:41). To whom were they

# Finding My Faith

added? The group of disciples of Jesus Christ. How were they added? They were baptized. A few verses later in Acts 2:47 it says, ". . . And the Lord added to the church daily those who were being saved." Saved people were being added daily to the church. Do you remember how they were being saved? It was repentance and baptism that saved them from their sins (Acts 2:38). According to the blueprint, you were only added to the Lord's church when you were baptized for the remission of your sins (see Gal. 3:26-29).

Acts 5:14 says, "And believers were increasingly added to the Lord, multitudes of both men and women." Acts 11:24 says, "a great many people were added to the Lord." At first glance, these two verses don't show how people were being added to the Lord's church. Why don't they? Well, why doesn't your cookie recipe tell you exactly how many eggs to use? It does. . . in the ingredients list. However, in the step by step instructions it already assumes you know how many eggs you will need.

Acts 2 is a Christian's ingredients list.

- The people were taught about Jesus (Acts 2:14-36).
- They believed and confessed Jesus (Acts 2:37).
- They realized their sin and wrongdoing (Acts 2:37).
- Peter's solution was given (repent and be baptized) (Acts 2:38).
- The people followed the solution (Acts 2:41).
- The people were added to the Lord (Acts 2:41, 47).

Those are the ingredients. When you get to Acts 5 and Acts 11 and people were "added to the Lord," we can conclude they followed the ingredients list. Why doesn't Luke, the writer of Acts, tell us they were baptized? He doesn't need to. Just like the baker can conclude how many eggs are needed in a recipe based off the ingredients list, so can the reader of Acts conclude what "added to the Lord" means from Acts 2.

The New Testament writers didn't stop there. Paul takes almost an entire chapter in Romans 6 to describe how baptism removes the sin from our life. Water baptism is the act of putting our old, sinful self to death, burying ourselves in water, and rising up out of the water. It's the mirror image of Jesus giving Himself to die on the cross, being buried for three days, then rising up from the dead. Baptism removes the sin.

106 • • • • • • • •

# Are All "Christians" Created Equal?

Paul again wrote in Galatians 3, "For you are all sons of God through faith in Christ Jesus. For as many of you as were baptized into Christ have put on Christ. There is neither Jew nor Greek, there is neither slave nor free, there is neither male nor female; for you are all one in Christ Jesus. And if you are Christ's, then you are Abraham's seed, and heirs according to the promise" (vv. 26-29). Paul says we only put on Christ when we have been baptized into Christ.

Peter, when talking about Noah being saved by water, says, "There is also an antitype that now SAVES US—baptism" (1 Pet. 3:21, emphasis mine). It seems to me, the closer I study God's blueprint, the more I see the necessity of baptism in order for me to be saved.

Countless numbers of people over the years have concluded that all one has to do to be saved and added to the Lord's group of believers is to "accept Jesus in your heart," then "say the Sinner's Prayer," in order to "have a personal relationship with Jesus," or "just believe." Unfortunately, none of those phrases are found anywhere in God's blueprint. Not even the *idea* of those phrases is found in Scripture. But I will tell you what is found, "Repent and let every one of you be baptized in the name of Jesus Christ for the remission of your sins" (Acts 2:38). Only when the blueprint is followed, can someone become a Christian and a follower of Christ.

**UP FOR DEBATE?**

For years, people have tried to diminish the necessity of baptism. For some reason, baptism has become a topic of debate. Peter's answer for sin in the New Testament was "repent, and let every one of you be baptized in the name of Jesus Christ FOR THE REMISSION OF SINS" (Acts 2:38, emphasis mine). How do I get my sins taken away? According to Peter: repent and be baptized. As we noticed above, Peter later wrote, "there is now an antitype that now saves us—baptism" (1 Pet. 3:21). It seemed pretty clear to the New Testament writers how one was added to the Lord: repent and be baptized. Peter also reminded us in Acts 2 that the promise of salvation from our sins was for "all who are afar off, as many as the Lord our God will call" (v. 39). He's talking about you and me!

It's also interesting that an Old Testament prophet talked about a day when "a fountain shall be opened for the house of David and for the inhabitant of Jerusalem, for sin and for uncleanness" (Zech. 13:1). A fountain (water) shall be opened for sin and for uncleanness. Doesn't that sound a lot like baptism?

# Finding My Faith

Baptism in the New Testament was for the specific purpose of washing away sins. Peter says it's not the actual removal of filth from our flesh, but the answer of a clean conscience before God (1 Pet. 3:21). Today, far too many people who consider themselves "Christians" have never been baptized. They are "Christian" in name only but have never had their sins washed away as Peter said in Acts 2:38 and 1 Peter 3:21. Many denominations who consider themselves "Christians" refer to baptism as an "outward showing of your inward faith." It's an act that is done later, after your salvation. Sometimes even months or years later. Again, following God's blueprint, we never see people wait to get baptized once they were taught about Jesus. Look at the list below. All were immediately baptized after hearing about how Jesus could save them from their sins.

- 3,000 souls on the Day of Pentecost (Acts 2:41)
- An Ethiopian Eunuch after being taught in his chariot (Acts 8:26-38)
- Saul (Paul) as soon as he was taught by Ananias (Acts 9)
- Cornelius and his household after they were taught by Peter (Acts 10:47-48)
- Lydia after she was taught by Paul (Acts 16:15)
- A Philippian jailer after he was taught by Paul (Acts 16:33)

Several others were baptized throughout the Scriptures and all of them happened immediately after they were taught about Jesus. When people understand the ingredients to the recipe, it's really easy to follow. When we have sin in our lives, Jesus is the only One who can save us. When we are buried in the waters of baptism, it cleanses our conscience and sins before God, and we can rise out of the water a brand-new person.

However, if baptism isn't necessary to become a Christian, why even do it? To profess my inner faith outwardly? Shouldn't that be done on a daily basis with how I speak, live and treat others? Peter said, "Repent, and be baptized in the name of Jesus Christ FOR THE REMISSION OF SINS" (Acts 2:38, emphasis mine). The blueprint seems pretty clear on the topic. When will we stop arrogantly making up new ways to follow Jesus and simply follow what He asks us to do?

## ARE ALL "CHRISTIANS" CREATED EQUAL?

Simply calling one's self a "Christian" does not make aperson a Christian. I can call myself the President of the United States, but that doesn't mean it's true. God's blueprint is very clear and specific on what it takes to be added to the Lord. So, to answer our question; no, not all "Christians" are created equal. How can you belong to Christ and be a follower of Christ if you have not followed His blueprint? You cannot be added to the Lord by raising your hand during a prayer, wishing to be saved, accepting Jesus in your heart, just simply believing (faith only), saying a specific prayer, or by any other scripturally foreign tradition.

Jesus says, "I am the way, the truth, and the life. No one comes to the Father except through Me" (John 14:6). If we want to be added to the Lord, we need to do it His way. If we want to seriously be considered a follower of Christ, we will truly follow Him. Christians should follow Christ. If a church, preacher, parents, friend, or anyone else teaches anything different than what Christ teaches . . . how can they truly follow Christ and be a Christian?

Being a Christian really comes down to one word: obedience. It's the same lesson that was taught through the Old Testament. If the people obeyed God, He promised to protect and save His people. If they didn't obey, there were consequences. The New Testament message is the same. We obey God by obeying the lifesaving Gospel of Jesus Christ (1 Cor. 15:2). The gospel that Jesus Christ died, was buried, and was raised from the dead. We obey that gospel when we die to sin, are buried under water in baptism, and rise from the water a saved person (Rom. 6).

One time my wife gave one of her recipes to a friend. It's a great recipe that our family loves. My wife followed up with our friend a few days later to see if her family liked the recipe as much as we do. The friend said, "It came out horrible. I won't be making that recipe again." When pressed a little further to make sure she followed the recipe, the friend said, "Well, I didn't have some of the ingredients, so I substituted some items for some similar ingredients." That was the problem! "Similar" is not the same as the real thing.

And that right there is what's wrong with many who consider themselves "Christians." What started as one recipe in Acts 2, has slowly been changed and been substituted for "similar" but different ingredients. It's no wonder there are 43,000 different types of churches who all consider themselves "Christian" (following Jesus). We've ruined

# Finding My Faith

God's recipe! We can't just substitute ingredients if we don't like what the recipe calls for. It's time we get back to truly following Jesus and His commands. You have the recipe . . . it's called the Bible. You've spent the first half of the book learning the recipe. Now it's time to actually use it. But don't forget to use it the right way!

# Are All "Christians" Created Equal?

## Chapter 10 Study Questions

1. What does the term "Christian" actually mean?

2. Where is the term first used in the Bible? What were they doing to call themselves Christians?

3. What does it mean to be "added to the Lord?" What was needed to be "added to the Lord?"

4. Reread Acts 2:36-38 and 1 Peter 1:21. Why do you think so many "Christians" try to avoid baptism?

5. What is the Gospel of Jesus Christ and how do we obey it today? (see 1 Cor. 15:1-4; Rom. 6).

# CHAPTER 11
# Using the Bible in My Congregation

Leaving the church building where I work, there are two main ways to get to my house. They both take just about the same amount of time and they are both about the same mileage. When I drive one way, I pass a lot of houses, a cemetery, and a couple of schools. When I go the other way, it's basically open fields with a few houses sprinkled in. When it comes to my drive home, there is no wrong decision. I guess it just depends on your preference of scenery. The destination is still the same, the journey is just a little different.

This is how many people view religion. There are an estimated 2.3 billion people in the world who consider themselves "Christians" and claim to follow the Bible.[1] Those 2.3 billion people are divided into 43,000 *different* (notice the emphasis on *different*) churches (see chapter 2). A common view among those claim to believe in Jesus is that we all follow the same Bible, so we are all headed to the same destination: heaven. It doesn't matter how we get there, all that matters is we get there.

At first glance, this doesn't seem like a bad idea. Thousands of people have "shopped around" to find the right church that fits their unique style and wants in life. It's not unusual to find families skip from church to church until they find one that is similar to their beliefs and opinions. The idea is that all who consider themselves "Christians" are going to heaven, we are all just taking different paths to get there. Just choose the one that best fits your preference.

Is this really the plan we see in the Bible? Is this what God intended for His church to be? Billions of people spread throughout thousands of denominations all doing different things? Is it really okay for different churches to believe and practice different things even if what they believe and practice is in direct contradiction to the Bible?

# Using the Bible in My Congregation

## WHAT IS THE CHURCH?

Church is a lot like the word "love." It means different things to different people. I love my wife. I also love hamburgers, but those are two very different kinds of love. To several, church is the building where people meet to worship. To others, church is what you do at the building. When I was little, I would "play church." To most people, church is a building full of boring people that follow the traditions and teachings of an old book. Recently, people have tried to make "church" fun and entertaining. They've added worship bands, comedians, children's church, playgrounds, skateparks, and a whole lot more trying to appeal to a younger audience.

Let me suggest to you that church is none of those things. If we are truly following the blueprint and finding our answers from God's word, we see the church is much more than a building and what happens at that building. The word "church" comes from the Greek word *ekklesia* which means, "an assembly or called out body." It's actually made up of two Greek words *ek*, which means "out of" and *kaleo* which means "to call." The church is literally the group or *assembly* of people who have been *called out* from sin and the world.

Our English word "church" also comes from the Greek, but from the word *kyriakos* which means, "belonging to the Lord." That's very similar to the meaning of Christian (belonging to or follower of Christ). In other words, you only become part of the Lord's church when you belong to Him. You're only added to the Lord through repentance and baptism (see chapter 10: "Are All 'Christians' Created Equal?" for more information).

Simply put, the church is the group of people who belong to Christ and have been added to Him. Church is not a building and it's not simply what we do at the building. Church is the people.

## PURPOSE OF THE CHURCH

Starting in Acts 2, we see over 3,000 believers group together and start worshiping God and following the doctrine of the apostles (Acts 2:42-47). As they continued to teach about Jesus and make disciples, the church continued to grow in number. Once all the believers left Jerusalem, Christians were scattered all over Europe, Asia, and Africa. The believers met together in local groups to worship God, but also to

# Finding My Faith

teach about Jesus Christ and make more disciples. Even in the earliest moments of the church, their purpose becomes clear. There are four main purposes of the Lord's church.

### Purpose #1: Worship

Worship is when we show praise and adoration for a higher being. In this case, it is praising God. Based on what we read in our New Testaments, the Christians were meeting on the first day of the week to worship and praise God together (Acts 20:7; 1 Cor. 16:1-2). They started meeting on Sunday because this was the day Jesus rose from the dead. This is important because one of the major aspects of New Testament worship is the Lord's Supper, which He instituted before He died (Matt. 26:26-29; Mark 14:22-25; Luke 22:19-20). He took unleavened bread and juice from the vine (wine) and instructed His apostles to eat and drink in remembrance of Him. It was a memorial of His death, burial, and resurrection. Paul reminds us of the significance and the meaning in 1 Corinthians 11:23-26. So, the disciples met on the first day of the week (Sunday), to remember the sacrifice Jesus made and take the Lord's Supper.

Yes, the Bible doesn't specifically say which Sunday to meet. Is it every Sunday? Once a month? Once a year? The Bible doesn't say. However, the Bible implies that the Christians were meeting *every* Sunday. Both Acts 20:7 and 1 Corinthians 16:1-2 suggest that this was normal practice for the disciples to meet on the first day of the week.

So, what did the disciples do while they were gathered together to worship on Sunday?

- **Observe the Lord' Supper** (Acts 20:7; 1 Cor. 11:23-26). As previously mentioned, the early disciples remembered the Lord's death, burial, and resurrection by eating the unleavened bread and drinking the fruit of the vine. Much like the Old Testament memorials, this was a memorial for the sacrifice that was made for the forgiveness of our sins.

- **Take up a collection** (1 Cor. 16:1-2). Paul directed the churches of Galatia, as well as the church in Corinth to collect some money to help the needy saints. More will be said on this topic later, but while the disciples were together worshiping, they took some time to collect some money for specific purposes.

# Using the Bible in My Congregation

- **Prayer** (1 Thess. 5:17; Eph. 6:18; Jas. 5:16; Phil. 4:6). Prayer is simply talking to God. There are countless verses in the Bible that talk about praying, but a few are listed above. Prayer is when we ask God for help, ask Him to help someone else, or simply thank Him. Prayer is a vital part of our relationship with God, just as communication with a spouse is vital to a marriage.

- **Preaching and Teaching** (Acts 11:26; 15:35; 18:11; 20:20) . A big part of our worship is teaching the gospel so others can be added to the Lord's church. We are also commanded to strengthen those who are already disciples. This is typically done in Bible classes and sermons, but it's also done in people's homes and in smaller groups.

- **Singing** (Matt. 26:30; Acts 16:25; Rom. 15:9; 1 Cor. 14:15; Eph. 5:19; Col. 3:16; Heb. 2:12; 13:15; Jas. 5:13). There is a reason I listed so many verses for singing. It's because these represent every time singing in worship and praise is mentioned in the New Testament. They all have one thing in common: no mechanical instruments of music are ever mentioned. All the music was made with the voices. Both individually and as a group of believers, the early disciples only sang in their worship to God. I know musical instruments are considered crucial to many churches today, but they weren't used in worship until Pope Vitalian I used an organ in AD 666. For over 600 years, the early church understood God's blueprint for worship said "*sing,*" and that means using our voices.

In regard to our worship, that's all we see in God's blueprint. Notice, we didn't see orchestras, rock bands, standup comedians, kids' church, schools supported by a church, plays, or any other forms of entertainment. I would suggest to you that if your local congregation is doing anything different or leaving any part of New Testament worship out of their regular services, then they are not following God's blueprint. Unfortunately, we don't get to choose the path toward our destination. God has given us the path. But we can choose whether or not to follow it (Matt. 7:13-14).

When the New Testament disciples gathered together, their purpose was to honor and praise God and remember a risen Savior. They were not there to entertain themselves. Their purpose was to worship!

### Purpose #2: Serve

It doesn't take long to read through the New Testament to see Jesus and His disciples had a passion for serving others. During His ministry, Jesus fed the multitudes, healed the sick, and loved the hopeless. That passion to serve carried over into the book of Acts as the New Testament church was beginning to take shape. Acts 2:45 says, "and they sold their possessions and goods, and divided them among all, as anyone had need" (NKJV). Acts 4:32-37 tell us that "there was not a needy person among them, for all who were owners of land or houses would sell them and bring the proceeds of the sales, and lay them at the apostles' feet; and they would be distributed to each, as any had need" (vs. 34-35, NASB).

As we mentioned earlier, the New Testament church was commanded to take up a collection of money when they were gathered together on the first day of the week. This money was given for a specific purpose. Paul said in 1 Corinthians 16:1-2, "Now concerning the collection FOR THE SAINTS. . ." (NKJV, emphasis mine). The money the churches collected was gathered up to help saints (other Christians) who were in need.

In Acts 11:27-30 we read about a famine that was going to happen throughout the world. "Then the disciples, each according to his ability, determined to send RELIEF TO THE BRETHREN dwelling in Judea" (Acts 11:29, emphasis mine). Again, the money that was collected by the local churches was used to help serve brethren (other Christians) who were in need.

As Paul was on his way to Jerusalem to "serve the saints" (Rom. 15:25), he reminds the readers of Romans that there were certain needs that should be met. He mentioned that churches in Macedonia and Achaia "have been pleased to make a contribution FOR THE POOR AMONG THE SAINTS in Jerusalem" (Rom. 15:26, emphasis mine). Again, the contribution that was collected was to help the saints (other Christians) who were in need.

Unfortunately, too many churches have missed the mark on this issue. Church money has been used to support institutions like colleges, schools, day care facilities, and children's homes. Church money is handed out to strangers needing help with rent, utility bills, and groceries. This is not how God's blueprint tells us to use the church contribution. Every time we see church money being used; it was to serve the needs *of the saints*.

Church money was also used to pay preachers and spread of the gospel. 1 Corinthians 9:14 says, "So also the Lord directed those who proclaim the gospel to get their living from the gospel" (NASB). Paul even received payment at different times throughout his preaching and teaching (Phil. 4:15-18). These are the only two areas where we see church money being used: helping needy saints and supporting the spread of the gospel.

Some churches have received a bit of a bad reputation for only "helping their own." Don't they care about strangers? Why can't the church help people who aren't Christians? Unfortunately, churches have also missed the mark on what it means to serve. Yes, the church money cannot be used to support institutions, schools, etc. And yes, according to the Bible, the church money cannot be used on someone who isn't a saint (a Christian). However, that does not take away our individual responsibility to serve all people.

Paul makes this distinction in Romans 12:13 when he wrote, "contributing to the needs of the saints, practicing hospitality." As he is listing attributes for healthy Christianity, Paul makes two very separate points: help the needy saints and practice hospitality. Hospitality is literally the act of serving strangers. This is why we call jobs in restaurants and hotels the "hospitality business," you are serving strangers.

Just because the church money cannot be used, doesn't mean we neglect to help those who are in need. Hebrews 13:2 says, "Do not neglect to show hospitality to strangers . . . ." The church money is collected to help the needy saints and the spread of the gospel, but as individual members of the church we shouldn't neglect to help those who are in need. This can be done in countless ways and is vital to the purpose of New Testament Christianity.

### Purpose #3: Fellowship

Fellowship is not a word that we use very often in our secular vocabulary, unless you are a *Lord of the Rings* fan. Fellowship comes from the idea of having commonality and communion with God and your surrounding community. Notice what the New Testament church was doing at its earliest stages: They were continued in the apostles' doctrine (Acts 2:42)—they all believed the same thing.

- They continued in fellowship (Acts 2:42)—they had a sense of community.

- They broke bread and prayed (Acts 2:42)—they worshiped together.

- They were all together and had all things in common (Acts 2:44)—they were unified.

- They sold property and possessions for sharing with those in need (Acts 2:45)—they made sure everyone's needs were met.

- Every day they were continuing with one mind in the temple, eating together in people's homes, and worshiping together (Act 2:46)—they were together daily, forming relationships.

- They did all this with gladness and simplicity of heart (Acts 2:46).

New Testament Christians genuinely enjoyed serving God and serving each other. They were a community and a family. Of course, with people there will be problems, but they worked through their problems for the greater good of the Lord's church. Their mission was to worship, serve, and have fellowship with each other, but all these purposes were leading toward their greatest purpose.

### Purpose #4: Save

In Matthew 28, Jesus left His apostles with some final commandments. "Go therefore and make disciples of all the nations, baptizing them in the name of the Father and of the Son and of the Holy Spirit, teaching them to observe all things that I have commanded you" (Matt. 28:19-20). In the last chapter we discussed how baptism is what saves us. Peter confirms this in 1 Peter 3:21. Jesus commanded His apostles to go into the entire world and teach the gospel of Christ and make disciples by baptizing them in the name of the Father, the Son, and the Holy Spirit.

# Using the Bible in My Congregation

As the four Gospels conclude and the New Testament church begins, the message of salvation remained the same. Salvation was only possible by repentance and baptism. In Acts 2, we see 3,000 souls added to the Lord's church. As the book of Acts continues, more and more souls were being saved. I often wondered why the message of Christ spread so fast. Why were so many people turning to Jesus and being added to the church? Why are we still talking about Jesus 2,000 years later? It's because of the simple command that Jesus gave us: teach and save.

The Lord's church will only continue to grow if we fulfill our purpose of saving the lost. This responsibility belongs to the church. It is our obligation to take the gospel into the world and teach about the sin cleansing power of Jesus Christ. Imagine for a moment that we find a cure for cancer. It doesn't matter the kind of cancer and it doesn't matter if it's in advanced stages; we would have the cure. Would you keep it to yourself? Of course not! We would share the cure with the entire world! We would save all of our friends and loved ones. We would rejoice knowing a cure was found.

Jesus is the cure. Not to cancer, but to something far worse: sin. Sin is killing us. Sin is dangerous, but Jesus can cure us. Why would we keep silent about Him? Why aren't we out spreading the good news of Jesus Christ? This was the main purpose of the early church. They wanted to take the message of Christ and share it with whoever would listen.

As members of the Lord's New Testament church, we should be equally motivated to share the message of Jesus. Our responsibility is to save the lost.

The more I study the Scriptures, the more I see how seriously God takes these four purposes of the church. We all need to be *saved* from our sins and have a relationship with Jesus. Once we realize how lost we were without Him, God deserves all our praise and *worship.* We join together with others who have been saved and form a bond of *fellowship.* Then we all work together to share the life-saving message of the gospel with all who need it.

Unfortunately, we can't cover every single issue and detail of the Lord's church. However, I wanted to share with you a few more points to consider. As the church began to grow in the New Testament, the individual members formed local congregations. These local places of worship served as smaller bodies of the Lord's church where worship, fellowship, service, and the work to save could be done on a more intimate scale. These local churches were autonomous. That means although they were all part of the overall body of saved believers, the individual churches were independent and self-governing. Peter told the elders to "shepherd the flock WHICH IS AMONG YOU" (1 Pet. 5:2, emphasis mine).

This means that the church is not a denomination. Many denominations have a governing board or a "main church or campus" that calls the shots for all the other "campuses." Each time the church (or churches) are addressed in Scripture, they are addressed as individual congregations.

These individuals are to be led by a group of men called elders, shepherds, pastors, bishops, or overseers. All these terms are used interchangeably (see 1 Pet. 5:1-4; Acts 20:17-28). Please note that a preacher and a pastor are not the same thing. Our secular religious world has morphed these two words into meaning the same thing, but God's word does not. A pastor is a shepherd, elder, and overseer—different names used for the same role. A man serving in this role must meet certain qualifications (1 Tim. 3:1-7; Titus 1:5-9). Also, a pastor does not lead a congregation alone (Titus 1:5). There is no "lead pastor" or lead elder. They all work together to lead God's local body. And, as already stated, they only serve the congregation of which they are a part (1 Pet. 5:2).

If you are looking for a congregation with which to worship and serve, I urge you, to consider what God's word says about the church and local congregations. Find one whose purpose is to worship, serve, fellowship, and save the way God intended. Find a congregation that follows the blueprint, doctrine, and teachings of Christ and the apostles (Acts 2:42). Find a congregation that doesn't have any other creed, book, or teachings as it's authority (Gal. 1:8; 2 Cor. 11:4; 2 John 1:10). Most of all, find a congregation where you can be an active participant in the Lord's Kingdom.

It's true that many churches and people who consider themselves "Christians" are on different paths, but not all paths lead to the same place. Unfortunately, there are too many congregations out there that look nice, have a fancy stage, fun music, and moving speakers, but they aren't following the blueprint of God's word. Too many people who consider themselves "Christians" have been fooled into worshiping and working with a church that's different than God designed. Do you remember the Old Testament themes that became the driving force of the Bible? Obedience, sacrifice, love, and salvation. All four principles are found in the four major purposes of the church. We worship God the way He wants to be worshiped: obedience. We serve God, each other, and strangers the way God has served us: sacrifice. We fellowship with one another and have a sense of community: love. We seek and save the lost, teaching them the gospel of Jesus Christ: salvation.

God had a plan from the very beginning. If you and I, as the church, are building upon the architect's plan, remember to build in God's way. Don't be persuaded to take a different path. Take God's path and it's sure to lead to heaven.

## Chapter 11 Study Questions

1. What is the church? How are you added to the church?

2. What are the four major purposes of the church? How are these connected to the Old Testament?

3. What are the five major components of worship? Why is it so important to make sure these are all present in our present-day congregations?

4. Describe fellowship. What are some ways you can grow closer with your fellow Christians?

5. What does it mean to be autonomous? Compare and discuss the differences between a denomination and an autonomous church.

6. Who leads the individual, local congregations of God's people? Why aren't they able to lead multiple churches?

7. Explain the difference between a pastor and a preacher.

# CHAPTER 12
# Don't Be Persuaded

If you've ever shopped for a new car, then you know the power of salesmen. As soon as you pull up to the lot, they are waiting for you like a pack of wild dogs. You can hardly get out of your car before they descend upon you like you're their next meal. As they start showing you potential new cars, it becomes clear they rarely care about you as the client, they are only wanting to sell a car and earn their commission. They will tell you whatever you want to hear as long as it means you will walk away spending as much money as possible. I can't even begin to tell you how many people I know who have walked away having not only paid too much for a brand-new car, but also having paid for the add-ons and service packages that cost far more than they're worth. It's because salesmen are really good at what they do. They say that a good salesman can sell ice to an Eskimo.

## RELIGIOUS SALESMEN

Unfortunately, there are religious salesmen out there. There are people who couldn't care less about what they are selling, so long as they can persuade you to join their side or follow their belief system. Instead of teaching the lifesaving gospel of Jesus Christ and the importance of following God's blueprint, they are selling their own church and their own agenda. They will tell you what you want to hear to make you feel good and accepted. They will change God's blueprint if it means making you happy. They will take away verses that step on toes and pierce our hearts. They will even add opinions and make them sound like truth. They will give you a place to "worship" that doesn't feel like "church" and they will do whatever it takes to keep you coming back. Sure, truth will be sprinkled in occasionally, but it becomes lost in the endless flow of half-truths and deceptions.

Paul mentioned this when he wrote, "For the time will come when they will not endure sound doctrine, but according to their own desires, because they have itching ears, they will heap up for themselves teachers; and they will turn their ears away from truth, and be turned aside to fables" (2 Tim. 4:3, NKJV). In other words, people will leave sound teaching and truth because they would rather be entertained, and they want preachers to make them feel good.

Most people believe church success can be measured by two factors: numbers and money. We want to know what church has the most members. Apparently, the number of members means greater success because the greater the number, the greater the contribution. In our society, we measure our success with the amount of money someone earns. We do the same with churches. The churches with the most members and the most money are obviously more successful. A church with 5,000 members is obviously a "better" church than a church with 50 members.

Let me say something that isn't very popular in our current religious society: God does not measure success on money and the number of people sitting in the pews. God measures success based on true discipleship. I firmly believe that a church of 50 members who are truly following God's blueprint is stronger than a church of 5,000 members that have disregarded the true teachings of the Bible. Sure, the church of 5,000 members might be doing good things, but don't forget what Jesus said, "Not everyone who says to me, 'Lord, Lord' shall enter the kingdom of heaven, but he who does the will of my Father in heaven" (Matt. 7:21). It's all about true discipleship.

**TRUE DISCIPLESHIP**

There are millions of people who claim to be "Christians," but do you remember what a Christian is? It's a disciple and a follower of Christ. Unfortunately, there are millions of people who claim to follow Christ because they give money to a church and sit in the pew a couple of times a week. God doesn't measure our spiritual success based on the size of congregations or their bank accounts. Our responsibility is to teach the word of God and make disciples (Matt. 28:19-20).

Jesus warned of people who would come teaching and practicing different things than what Jesus commanded. He told us to beware of false prophets, "who come to you in sheep's clothing, but inwardly they are ravenous wolves" (Matt. 7:15). They look and sound good, but they will tear you apart.

# Don't Be Persuaded

Jesus even mentions the devastating reality of not following God's blueprint when He said, "Not everyone who says to Me, 'Lord, Lord,' shall enter the kingdom of heaven, but he who does the will of My Father in heaven. Many will say to Me in that day, 'Lord, Lord, have we not prophesied in Your name, cast our demons in Your name, and done many wonders in Your name?' And then I will declare to them, 'I never knew you; depart from Me, you who practice lawlessness!" (Matt. 7:21-23).

Unfortunately, there will be people claiming to be Christians, but they have not truly followed Christ. Sure, they've done a lot of wonderful things in the name of Jesus, but they weren't following God's will. There are countless numbers of congregations, denominations, and individual Christians who do a lot of good for our society. There are a lot of people who are helpless sheep with pure hearts, being led by ravenous wolves. There are good people who are doing good things in the name of Jesus. However, the reality is that we have a responsibility not just to make people love Jesus; we must teach people to follow Him too!

True discipleship comes not only when we love Jesus but when we follow His every word. Jesus Himself told us, "If you love Me, keep My commandments" (John 14:15). This means we need to pay very close attention to how we worship, where we worship, what our church teaches and practices, but also how I live on a daily basis. True discipleship should overtake every aspect of our professional, private, religious, and family lives.

## DON'T BE PERSUADED

There have always been people who will look for the latest and greatest in the religious community. We are always looking for the latest fad and biggest congregations. We are looking for a preacher who make us feel good and won't step on our toes. We look for kids' programs (even if we don't see any in the Bible) and we look for a congregation on the cutting edge. We want to be entertained. We want to be excited to come to services and often that's by way of movie nights, concerts, or comedians.

I have found that there are several factors that go into someone giving up on God's blueprint and doing things God's way.

The first is **persuasion**. Satan is real and he is powerful. He can persuade us to do almost anything. Satan is very good at making sin look fun. He makes different religions and denominations sound right. He supports different philosophies that try to persuade people away from God. I believe Satan works through college professors, bosses, significant others, protestors on college campuses, coworkers, friends, and family members. Satan works through media, entertainment, and pop culture. He is working in your mind as we speak. Everything we see and experience on a daily basis is trying to persuade us in one direction or another. Satan is very good at persuading us away from following God.

Don't believe me? Why do you think there are so many different philosophies, religions, and denominations? Why do you think we have protests about abortions and homosexuality? It's because Satan is real and he is persuading people to think and act in ways that are contrary to God's word. Jesus even said, "for false christs and false prophets will rise and show great signs and wonders to deceive, if possible, even the elect" (Matt. 24:24). Yes, Satan is even working in the church and among God's people.

Another reason people give up on God is because of a **lack of confidence**. Maybe you are new to the Bible. You feel like you haven't read or studied enough. You don't know where you should stand on moral, political, and religious issues. Maybe you hear a friend or college professor give a compelling argument against God and religion and now you don't know what to believe. More and more people are giving up on God because they just aren't confident in what they believe.

This leads to people being **ashamed** of what they believe. Sadly, our society has a way of shaming people who don't act and think a certain way. If you don't agree with Hollywood and pop culture, you are a bigot. If you disagree with abortion and homosexuality, then you are hateful and judgmental. Satan will do anything to make you feel ashamed of God. So, the easy thing to do is give up on God and fit right in with society. John wrote, "Nevertheless even among the rulers many believed in Him, but because of the Pharisees they did not confess Him, lest they should be put out of the synagogue; for they loved the praise of men more than the praise of God" (John 12:42-43).

We have all been guilty of **selfishness** at times. Remember our earlier verse from 2 Timothy when it says people will turn away from sound doctrine because of their own desires? They will have itching ears. They will want to be entertained. Let's make one thing clear: Christianity is about giving up our own desires and giving our lives in service to God (Luke 9:23).

# Don't Be Persuaded

Lastly, some people leave God's blueprint simply out of **ignorance**. Peter told us this would happen when speaking of Paul's writings he said, ". . . in all his epistles, speaking in them of these things, in which are some things hard to understand, which untaught and unstable people twist to their own destruction, as they do all the rest of the Scriptures" (2 Pet. 3:16). The Bible is very easy to twist and manipulate. I can take anything in the Bible and make it say what *I* want it to say. I can take things out of context and twist Scripture and make you believe some pretty wild things, but that doesn't mean I'm right.

Unfortunately, this is how people handle God's blueprint. Untaught and unstable people twist the words of the Bible. They're ignorant. In the introduction I gave you a real-life example of my own ignorance. When arguing against homosexuality, it was brought to my attention that the Bible also teaches against eating pigs and shellfish (Lev. 11). In my ignorance, I was almost persuaded to believe the Bible could not be completely followed. In my ignorance, I was letting an internet troll who knew nothing about God's blueprint, persuade me to question God's word.

However, through reading and studying, I quickly found out that Leviticus is under the Old Law while you and I live under the New Law (see chapters 5-7). Under the New Law, pigs and shellfish can be eaten (Acts 10). Yet, under the New Law, homosexuality is still a sin (Rom. 1:18-32; 1 Cor. 6:9-10).

Sadly, Satan has and will continue to persuade too many people, even Christians, away from truly following God's will (Matt. 7:21-23). He will use any tactic he can to get to us and tear us apart. He is a wolf in sheep's clothing. He will attack our confidence and make us feel ashamed. He will bring out our selfish desires and feed off our ignorance. Satan is smart and powerful; and he is winning. It's up to us to make sure we recognize his attacks and learn to fight against him.

## DON'T GIVE UP

Fighting Satan is not easy. He's relentless and he is strong, but we do have some pretty powerful tools in our arsenal. Let's not forget who is on our side. God told Joshua as he was preparing to lead the children of Israel into battle, "Have I not commanded you? Be strong and of good courage; do not be afraid, nor be dismayed, for the Lord your God is with you wherever you go" (Josh. 1:9). Don't forget that our awesome,

# Finding My Faith

all-powerful God is on *our* side. He has commanded us to be strong and courageous. Yes, Satan is trying to devour and tempt us, but God is with us wherever we go. Perhaps Paul said it best, "If God is for us, who can be against us?" (Rom. 8:31).

It's also important to stay diligent and continue growing in God's word. Of course, it's easy to be persuaded away from God when we aren't constantly meditating on God's word (Psa. 1). Just like the athlete who will lose his competitive edge once he stops training, we lose our will to fight Satan when we stop growing in God's word.

The Christians in Berea should be a great example to us. When Paul and Silas were teaching the Bereans about Christ, they would then go search the Scriptures to figure whether or not Paul and Silas were telling the truth (Acts 17:11). Christianity would look very different if all Christians simply open their Bibles and test what their preachers, pastors, elders, and teachers are saying. It's very easy for pastors and preachers to look nice on a Sunday, put together a fancy presentation, and speak an encouraging message, but that doesn't make what they are teaching accurate.

The greatest tool we have is the ability to open our Bibles and test the words we hear from others. That's why we spent the first half of this book understanding our Bibles. If we don't understand them, how can we use them to strengthen our faith and make sure truth is being taught? Peter told his readers to continue to "grow in the grace and knowledge of our Lord and Savior Jesus Christ" (2 Pet. 3:18). We need to continue to grow and study!

Paul told Timothy to "Be diligent to present yourself approved to God, a worker who does not need to be ashamed, rightly dividing the word of truth" (2 Tim. 2:15). We have the responsibility not only to study God's word but to use it correctly. The term "rightly divide" is an old farming term used when the farmer had to plow his fields in long, straight lines. Plowing your field in crooked lines not only looks tacky, but it doesn't best utilize the space. Straight lines, spaced adequately apart, give the farmer the biggest harvest possible. God's word is the same. Twisting the Scriptures won't get us very far on our journey to heaven. Making crooked lines of God's word deceives the listeners and is sinful. Test everyone and make sure truth is being taught.

# Don't Be Persuaded

I want to end this chapter with one last piece of advice: don't be ashamed of your faith. In our verse above, Paul reminded Timothy not to be ashamed of God's word and to present himself approved by God. We spend too much time trying to gain the approval of our family and friends. We spend too much time worrying about what the famous actors and athletes think and believe. When our faith and beliefs don't lineup with the popular opinion, we feel ashamed and are more likely to give up on our faith.

Our society has grown accustomed to shaming those who don't believe the popular opinion. Unfortunately, Christianity is growing less popular. Don't be ashamed of our God or His word. And most importantly, don't be ashamed of living the life of a disciple. Don't let Satan and this world persuade you to give up on living for Christ and following God's will. It's God's approval we seek, not man's.

Paul boldly said, "For I am not ashamed of the gospel of Christ, for it is the power of God to salvation for everyone who believes, for the Jew first and also for the Greek" (Rom. 1:16). Don't be ashamed of the one who has given salvation. If there was one thing Paul was persuaded about, it was his commitment to Christ. He said, ". . . I am not ashamed, for I know whom I have believed and am persuaded that He is able to keep what I have committed to Him until that Day" (2 Tim. 1:12). When you are truly convinced and convicted that Jesus Christ is the Son of God and you want to give your life to Him through repentance and baptism, there should be nothing that can persuade you away from His love and power. We don't need to be ashamed of what we believe because we have a Savior who is going to bring us home to heaven.

## TIME TO MAKE A CHOICE

When Joshua was finishing the conquest of Canaan, he gathered all the people and gave one of the greatest speeches in the Bible. He reminded the people that God has delivered them into the Promised Land and has continued to take care of them. He closes his speech with this simple choice: "Now therefore, fear the LORD, serve Him in sincerity and in truth, and put away the gods which your fathers served on the other side of the River and in Egypt. Serve the LORD! And if it seems evil to you to serve the LORD, choose for yourselves this day whom you will serve, whether the gods which your fathers served that were on the other side of the River, or the gods of the Amorites, in whose land you dwell. But as for me and my house, we will serve the LORD" (Josh. 24:14-15).

# Finding My Faith

Choose. It's time to make a choice. You either take a stand and serve the Lord or you choose to disregard the Bible and all its teachings. We can't keep one foot in the door and the other still standing outside. Joshua boldly and unashamedly chose God. Will you do the same? Or will you be like Agrippa who told Paul, "You almost persuade me to become a Christian" (Acts 26:28)? Almost is not good enough. It's time to go all in. It's time to follow the examples of faith we read about in the Bible. Yes, there are enemies of Christ who will always try to pull you away. Paul reminds us that their attempts to persuade people away from Christ are selfish and eternally deadly (Phil. 3:19).

However, our citizenship is in heaven. That's where we belong and it's where God wants us. Don't be persuaded by the religious salesmen of our day who tell you anything to join "their" church. Don't be persuaded by the latest and greatest fad. Test the words of preachers and "pastors." Stand firm in the teachings of the Bible. Only be persuaded of one thing: Jesus Christ rose from the dead and deserves our complete commitment.

# Don't Be Persuaded

## Chapter 12 Study Questions

1. Discuss some factors that make a church "successful." According to the New Testament, what makes a church successful?

2. There are thousands of churches who all think they are doing things the right way. What are some ways you can make sure you individually, and also your congregation, are following God's blueprint?

3. Discuss what true discipleship looks like according to Scripture. Why do you think so many people call themselves disciples, but don't live the life of a disciple?

4. What are some of the biggest factors persuading people away from Christ? Who is ultimately responsible for this?

5. What are some practical ways to take your stand for Christ? What can you do to show God you are not ashamed?

# CHAPTER 13
# Is My Faith Strong Enough?

Christians all over the world struggle with their faith. They wonder if they know enough, did they study enough, do they truly believe in God and His Son? People who have been Christians their whole life find themselves doubting God in times of trouble and hardships. We question God when things go wrong and we begin to doubt His love, mercy, and grace. Can I really be saved when I've done so many things wrong? Is salvation real?

We look at men and women like Abraham, Moses, Joseph, Ruth, Esther, Peter, and Paul and wonder if we could ever live up to their kind of faith. Can we ever have the kind of faith that will move mountains (Matt. 17:20) or close the mouth of a lion (Heb. 11:33)? Will I ever truly be able to let go of the sins and temptations of this world and completely give myself over to serving Christ? Is my faith strong enough to conquer my giants, deal with my hardships, and get me to heaven?

## DOUBTING OUR FAITH

Unfortunately, too many Christians are struggling in their faith. Studies have shown that a majority of people who consider themselves "Christians" have some doubt about their faith or their salvation. A Pew Research survey in 2007 showed that 83% of millennials (those born in the 1980s and 90s) said they *never* doubted God's existence. Now, that number has dropped to 68%. In a little over ten years, that number has dropped 15%. Now there are 32% of our young people who are doubting God.

Also, according to Pew Research, of those who consider themselves "Christians":

- 23% don't have an absolute certain belief in God. So, almost a quarter of them are not absolutely sure there is a God.

- 32% don't view their religion as very important in their lives. It's no coincidence that 32% of them admit to praying less than weekly and 55% admit to reading their Bibles less than once per week (which is typically on a Sunday, when and if they attend a church service).
- 67% will seldom participate in a worship service or organized Bible study.
- 14% either don't believe in heaven or don't know if it exists
- 30% don't believe in hell.

*Pew Research Center: Religious and Public Life*[1]

It is no wonder that churches are dying! This research shows people who consider themselves "Christians," and claim to love and obey Christ, are unsure of their belief in God, don't find religion important, are praying less than once per week, reading their Bibles less than once per week, aren't attending a church service or Bible study, and don't even know if heaven and hell are real! If heaven and hell aren't real, then what is the point of believing in God and following Christ? We might as well be living our lives with no moral code.

This worldly "Christianity" is dying and it's because those who consider themselves "Christians" are growing more and more unsure about who and what they believe.

**BLIND FAITH**

Steve Hayner, Professor at Columbia Theological Seminary, works with young people on a daily basis. He was asked what he believed were the causes of doubt and lack of faith in so many of our young people.[2] First, he found people were too distracted with other things to give enough attention to their relationship with Christ. As a preacher, I have found this to be true of many people, but especially young families. It seems young families have no problem putting in hours at the ballfield but will complain if a church service is fifteen minutes past the appropriate time. We will make sure our children never miss a ball game, homework assignment, or a recital, but we make Bible study and "extra" church services optional. If our child forgets his or her homework, we will drive all the way back home to get it for them, but it's okay to leave their Bible at home for Bible class. We will break our backs trying to make them the top seller in their class for the school fundraiser but teaching them to talk to others about Christ is too much for them. They can memorize the lines to their favorite cartoons but reciting a memory verse is too much to ask. Unfortunately, there are too many other distractions that are taking our focus away from Christ.

Second, Hayner found that there were many people who thought is was too difficult to start living a new life because of their faith. What was familiar to them was no longer familiar. People are uncomfortable with change. Jesus told us if we want to be His disciples, we must deny ourselves, pickup our cross, and follow Him (Luke 9:23). Denying ourselves the life we've always lived is a huge undertaking. It means giving up certain sins we enjoy, giving up friends we love, and giving up a lifestyle to which we've grown accustomed. Too many people are unwilling to part with the life they've always known. Faith in Christ was just too difficult for them.

Third, most people found a relationship with Christ was inconvenient. One person was quoted as saying, "losing my faith was a nice way to justify some bad decisions." Isn't it sad that most people will give up their faith simply because they would rather live a life of sin? If the Bible condemns the lifestyle they wish to live, it's easier to give up on God and the Bible than to give up their friends and lifestyle choices.

Sadly, even many New Testament Christians don't have a strong faith and lack confidence in themselves and the God they serve. Too many are questioning whether or not their faith is strong enough. Christians all over the world are walking through life, grasping at the air hoping to find God. It's as if they are blind and they are trying to find the light. However, once the light of Jesus Christ is revealed to them, they don't like where the light is leading them. They close their eyes even tighter so the light can't creep in.

Just as a blind person reaches for some sense of security, Christians are giving up on their faith in search of acceptance from a sinful world. They know God is there, they just aren't willing to see Him.

**MAKING PROGRESS**

When I was a young preacher working in San Jose, CA, one of the members of the church trained police dogs. These were huge, pure bread German Shepherds. I was invited to his house one Saturday afternoon and upon arriving, he was in the middle of a training session. Several dogs were out of their crates, playing in the yard. They all seemed happy while they played in the open grass. They were jumping around, wagging their tails, and playing with toys. However, when the command was given, the demeanor of these dogs changed. They became quiet and their ears perked up. They all fell in line next to their trainer. The once playful dogs were now quiet, standing at attention.

Just then, a man came out in a fat, padded body suit. He stood about twenty yards away from the dogs. As another command was given, one of the bigger dogs ran at a full sprint toward the man in the body suit. Teeth were showing and the barking could be heard from blocks away. It was a matter of seconds before that dog had grabbed onto the man's arm, pulled him down to the ground, and held him there, twisting and turning his head back and forth until he was commanded to release him. Then the dog pranced joyfully back to the trainer and received his treat for a job well done.

I had never experienced anything like that before. One moment, these huge dogs were playing and barking while having fun in the yard. The next moment, they were bringing down a full-grown man. The look in their eyes and the sound in their throat could only be described as fierce. It was scary but fascinating at the same time. These huge creatures were professionally trained. They had been taught from the time they were playful puppies to do their job with fierceness and intensity. I'm sure as puppies, when those dogs chased that man in the padded suit, there were more licks and kisses than growling and biting. But over time, once the training set in; the dogs had purpose. When their time came to leave the training facility, their jobs were to save lives with their fellow human police officers.

This is how I view our faith as Christians. We start as untrained and unsure newborn babes in Jesus Christ. In fact, Hebrews tells us that when we are "unskilled in the word of righteousness" we are babies needing only the milk of the word (Heb. 5:13). However, there comes a time when our faith needs to grow, no longer needing milk, but the solid food of the word.

At the beginning of our life of faith, we are just like those innocent puppies. We are playful, naive, and full of youth. Spiritual distractions will be easier to follow. It is natural to give up on our faith when we are met with struggles. It's easy to leave our faith because the lifestyle is difficult and unsure. But those puppies didn't become police dogs overnight. They trained every day. They worked and labored, making mistakes along the way. Their licks and kisses slowly turned into nibbles, and eventually turned into a strong bite able to take down a full-grown man.

Our faith must make progress. Moses didn't lead the children of Israel until he was eighty years old. Eighty years of mistakes, doubt, and fear. Abraham didn't see the promise of a son until he was one hundred years old. Paul spent the first half of his life murdering Christians. We won't become men and women of great faith overnight. It will take years of training. Struggles will come and sin will creep in, but progress means we are constantly moving forward. Then one day, we are strong enough to confidently walk with God.

**FIERCE FAITH**

You may be questioning and doubting your faith. Your faith may not even yet truly belong to you. Maybe it still belongs to your mom and dad, your preacher, or your elders. You may feel distracted and pulled in thousands of different directions. You may feel as if your spiritual life is inconvenient and unfamiliar. But it's time to grow up. It's time to stop playing around with your faith and turn your spiritual life into something fierce. Jesus tells us that if we only have the faith of a mustard seed, then we can move mountains (Matt. 17:20). It's time we learn how to start moving mountains:

- **Decide what you are passionate about.** After they conquered the Promise Land, Joshua reminded the children of Israel they couldn't serve God and the gods of their enemies. He made them choose. Jesus reminds us we cannot serve two masters (Matt. 6:24). We must make the most important decision of our lives: God or everything else? When we are passionate about God, nothing else becomes a distraction. Our faith becomes the most important aspect of our lives. More important than school, sports, hobbies, and even family.

- **Stop comparing yourself to others.** I was a hotshot athlete in elementary and middle school. I was knocked down a few pegs when I wasn't starting in football my freshman or sophomore years of high school. I never even got an offer to play football in college. That's because there is always someone better. Spiritually, it's not fair to compare ourselves to everyone around us. Moses can't be compared to Joseph. Abraham can't be compared to Timothy. Paul can't be compared to James. They were all special to God because they were all faithful. You can't be compared to Moses. You are special because *you* are faithful to God.

- **Make progress.** We live in a reality TV world. If you aren't the best, you get voted off. Spiritually that isn't the case. God never asked us to be the best, but He does want us to be *our* best. That means we continue making spiritual progress (Heb. 5:12-6:1). If we aren't growing, we are dying. Open your Bibles, talk to God in prayer, attend church services, get active in God's kingdom, live faithfully. You won't be perfect, but your mistakes will shape you into the spiritual warrior God knows you can be.

- **Be fierce.** Make no excuses for being passionate about your faith. Don't be embarrassed or distracted. Don't let others pull you away from what you know to be right. Let your passion for Christ push you forward in your spiritual journey. Go win souls, move mountains, and set the world on fire. We can do great things in God's kingdom.

I have known lots of spiritually strong Christians in my lifetime. They are spiritual giants in whom I put my complete trust. What's interesting is not one of them would consider themselves strong in the faith. They are all humble enough to admit their downfalls and their shortcomings. Yes, every Christian has wondered if his or her faith is strong enough, but only the strong will recognize the need to work harder.

Before I left the church member's house that day, he asked if I wanted to meet one of the dogs. Of course, he went and picked the large one that earlier had charged the padded man. He said, "Kevin, do you trust me?" "Of course," I replied. He said, "Stand very still and whatever you do, don't move." My friend held the leash and asked the dog to sit. The dog sat five feet away, staring at me with big, brown, playful eyes. With one command, the dog's hair raised on the back of his neck, his teeth were showing, and a deep growl came from his throat. His eyes never left mine. Another command and the dog barked, the deepest, loudest bark I had ever heard. As I stepped backward, the dog took one step closer, never taking his eyes off mine.

# Finding My Faith

"Don't move," my friend said. With another command, the dog sat back down and started wagging his tail. This dog was trained to attack, and I was his focus. I saw it in his eyes. He was not letting me get away. If commanded, the dog would have leaped toward me and clamped down on my arm. Thankfully, I trusted my friend.

I had never witnessed anything like that before. The dog had a laser focus on one thing: me. His eyes never left mine. I watched his eyes switch from fun and playful to fierce and determined.

Spiritually, we've been commanded to live every day for Jesus Christ (Luke 9:23). It's time we train ourselves to become fierce and determined disciples for the Lord, with a laser focus on serving Christ in every aspect of our lives. We must not let ourselves get distracted and turn away to meaningless worldly things. Don't compare your faith to anyone else. Instead, keep your eyes fiercely focused on Jesus Christ (Heb. 12:1-2).

No matter where you are on your spiritual journey, your faith is strong enough to do amazing things for God's kingdom. Now let's go move mountains.

# Is My Faith Strong Enough?

## Chapter 13 Study Questions

1. More and more "Christians" are not opening their Bibles, not praying, and not attending worship services. Why do you think that is?

2. Steven Hanner, professor of theology, had some ideas for why young people are leaving their faith. Why do you think young people are leaving their faith? What can you do to stop this trend?

3. Besides your faith, what are you passionate about? How do these passions compare to your passion for Christ?

4. List some characteristics of fierce faith. Name some characters in the Bible with fierce faith? Can you think of anyone in your personal life with fierce faith? Look at those names and characteristics. Memorize them. Repeat them daily. Now choose every day to live like those spiritual giants.

5. Where do you think your faith is currently? What can you do to start making progress towards fierce faith?

# Conclusion

This book was not designed to be some grand, new take on Faith. It was not designed to give you all the facts or give you everything you'll ever need for your spiritual journey. Only the Bible contains everything you will need to succeed in life and godliness (2 Pet. 1:3). However, I hope this book helped you in some small way to realize your worth within God's family.

Your faith is one of the most precious gifts you've been given. Your faith is what holds you close to your Creator and what keeps you moving forward in times of trouble. Jesus says, "I am the way and the truth and the life. No one comes to the Father except through Me" (John 14:6, NKJV). Faith in Jesus is the only way to heaven. Sure, there will be other religions who say different, but if this book has taught us anything, it's that the Bible is truth. The Bible tells us Jesus is the way to the Father.

We have been given the opportunity to be united with Jesus through the waters of baptism. Again, other religions, even some who consider themselves "Christians," will teach baptism isn't necessary. However, we must get our beliefs from the Bible, not other religions or churches. Peter says baptism saves us (1 Pet. 3:21). Paul reminds us we become a new person once we have died with Christ in baptism (Rom. 6). Peter preaches that we need to repent and be baptized "for the remission of sins" (Acts 2:38). Even Jesus commanded it in Matthew 28:19-20. I've been saved by God's grace (Eph. 2:9). Without God's grace, He would never have sent Jesus and it's because of Jesus, I have eternal life with my heavenly Father waiting for me.

This book was designed to help you dig deeper into finding and understanding your faith. We spent the first half getting to know our Bibles and the words God gave to us. Without first understanding the instruction manual, you'll never learn how to build the product properly.

# Conclusion

The second half of the book was spent learning how to use the Bible that's been given to us.

Your spiritual journey may only be beginning. This book is just a simple tool to get you to your final destination. The faith that you are cultivating is something that will, Lord willing, be with you for eternity. James 2:14-26 tells us that our faith needs to be a working one. Our actions and words should reflect the faith that has been planted inside our hearts. Our faith should motivate us to work in God's kingdom and do amazing things with God's people.

I would like to leave you with one last request: don't keep your faith to yourself. We are commanded to go into the world and teach others about our faith in Jesus Christ (Matt. 28:19-20). In Acts 26:1-29, we read about how Paul felt compelled to dedicate his life to spread the gospel and build faith in others. He, along with several others in the New Testament, dedicated his life to share the soul saving message of Jesus Christ.

Imagine for a moment, that you discover the cure to cancer. What do you do with it? Do you keep it to yourself, only saving the ones close to you? Or do you share it with the world, knowing that millions of people can be saved with your cure? I hope the answer is simple: share the cure.

Sadly, sin is far more deadly than cancer. The good news is there's a cure. Use your faith to build faith in others (Matt. 5:13-16). Use your faith to encourage others to do good and follow Jesus (1 Thess. 5:11). Use your faith to save other souls and bring them to Jesus Christ (1 Tim. 4:12-16).

Some people who read this book will be a young Christian or someone who is simply wanting to learn more about the Bible. My prayer for you is to let these words draw you closer to God. I hope this book can spark a flame within you to read the Scriptures and learn more about who our awesome God is. Turn to Him and give Him your life.

Others who read this book will be Christians who are either struggling or even advanced in spiritual wisdom. I pray that no matter where are in your spiritual journey, you can find words in this book to further deepen your faith. At the very least, maybe it was a review of things you already knew, but now it's our turn to share these faith

# Finding My Faith

changing chapters with someone who needs them. When you're truly convicted of who Jesus is and His power to save, you will have trouble keeping it to yourself.

The journey of faith is long and hard. Jesus reminds us that few will be able to persevere and finish (Matt. 7:13-14). No one else can walk your journey for you. So, go, find your faith. Strengthen it. Cherish it. Share it. And don't forget, "If God is for us, who can be against us?" (Rom. 8:31).

# Notes

## Introduction

[1]   Earls, Aaron, "Most Teenagers Drop out of Church as Young Adults," *LifeWay Research,* 15 January 2019, https://lifewayresearch.com/2019/01/15/most-teenagers-drop-out-of-church-as-young-adults/.

[2]   Ross, Bobby Jr., "Churches of Christ in Decline: US Culture to Blame?" *The Christian Chronicle,* 1 April 2015, https://christianchronicle.org/church-in-decline-u-s-culture-to-blame/.

## Chapter 1: The Journey Begins

[1]   Definition from *Oxford Languages Dictionary*

## Chapter 2: What Is "My Faith?"

[1]   "U.S. Public Becoming Less Religious," *Pew Research Center,* 3 November 2015, https://www.pewforum.org/2015/11/03/u-s-public-becoming-less-religious/.

## Chapter 3: Building a Castle

[1]   Walter, Kerry, "Faith Matters: Christian Mosaic," *The Daily Item,* 30 April 2015, https://www.dailyitem.com/opinion/faith-matters-christian-mosiac/article_2eeb36c4-ef6f-11e4-8fc2-378bd5bdedd7.html.

## Chapter 4: Understanding the Bible

[1]   Fahmy, Dalia, "Among Religious 'Nones,' Atheists and Agnostics Know the Most about Religion," *Pew Research Center,* 21 August 2019, https://www.pewresearch.org/fact-tank/2019/08/21/among-religious-nones-atheists-and-agnostics-know-the-most-about-religion/.

# Finding My Faith

### Chapter 9: Building My Spiritual Life

[1] "U.S. Public Becoming Less Religious," *Pew Research Center*, 3 November 2015, https://www.pewforum.org/2015/11/03/u-s-public-becoming-less-religious/.

### Chapter 11: Using the Bible in My Congregation

[1] Conrad Hackett and David McClendon, "Christians Remain World's Largest Religious. Group, but They Are Declining," *Pew Research Center*, 5 April 2017, https://www.pewresearch.org/fact-tank/2017/04/05/christians-remain-worlds-largest-religious-group-but-they-are-declining-in-europe/.

### Chapter 13: Is My Faith Strong Enough?

[1] "Young Adults Around the World Are Less Religious by Several Measures," *Pew Research Center*, 13 June 2018, https://www.pewforum.org/2018/06/13/young-adults-around-the-world-are-less-religious-by-several-measures/.

[2] "What If I Doubt My Faith?" *InterVarsity*, https://studentsoul.intervarsity.org/doubt-my-faith.

# About the Author

Kevin Harrington graduated from Florida College with his Bachelor of Arts in Biblical Studies with a minor in History in 2010. He has gone on to preach in congregations in Indiana, Nevada, California, and is currently the evangelist at Marion Street Church of Christ in Athens, AL.

Kevin, his wife, Brooke, and their son, Landon, moved to Alabama in 2014. Since then, they've welcomed another son, Eli, and adopted two children, Wilson and Hadley.

CPSIA information can be obtained
at www.ICGtesting.com
Printed in the USA
LVHW050713010721
691628LV00009B/212